RED STATE UPRISING

RED STATE UPRISING

HOW TO TAKE BACK
AMERICA

ERICK ERICKSON

Editor of RedState.com

AND LEWIS K. UHLER

Founder and President of the National Tax Limitation Committee

Since 1947
REGNERY
PUBLISHING, INC.
An Eagle Publishing Company • Washington, DC

Cataloging-in-Publication data on file with the Library of Congress

ISBN 978-1-59698-626-8

Published in the United States by
Regnery Publishing, Inc.
One Massachusetts Avenue, NW
Washington, DC 20001

www.regnery.com

Manufactured in the United States of America

10 9 8 7 6 5 4 3 2 1

Books are available in quantity for promotional or premium use. Write to Director of Special Sales, Regnery Publishing, Inc., One Massachusetts Avenue NW, Washington, DC 20001, for information on discounts and terms or call (202) 216-0600.

Distributed to the trade by:
Perseus Distribution
387 Park Avenue South
New York, NY 10016

To my parents, & to my wife
and children, all with love.
For freedom.
Heb. 11: 13-16

Erick Erickson

To my wife Cindy, and to our sons, and our
grandchildren who deserve an America
much more free and dynamic than
the one we are confronting today

Lewis K. Uhler

TABLE OF CONTENTS

REALITY CHECK

They're all terrible. All of them. Democrats. Republicans. The so-called "leaders" of both parties do nothing but compromise away our freedoms. The good guys are few and far between and need reinforcements.

Ask yourself a simple question: when is the last time the Democrats compromised in favor of the free market? Can't think of one? That's because it rarely happens. It's always the Republicans who compromise in favor of big government.

George W. Bush gave us steel tariffs in Pennsylvania, No Child Left Behind, the prescription drug benefit, TARP, and the auto bailout. His father before him gave us his lips on which we read a lie. They, like so many other Republicans, paraded around in conservative's clothing while having little in common with actual conservatives.

The Republicans gave us progressivism (read up on Robert LaFollette and Teddy Roosevelt). The Republicans gave us the Environmental Protection Agency. Heck, Republicans gave us Earl Warren, Nelson Rockefeller, Dede Scozzafava, Charlie Crist, and the list goes on and on and on.

The Democrats, by contrast, have given us over to European socialism, degenerated our moral society, destroyed the nuclear family, never met a race they didn't bait, and mushroomed the GOP's spending programs.

For too long the Republican Party has decided to be the Democrat-lite party, and the American voters in 2008 decided just to go with the real thing. Turns out, there is a difference between the Republican Party and the Democrat Party. While both may be terrible, the Democrats are worse.

Therein lies the terrible conundrum for voters. We're not choosing the lesser of two evils. We are choosing between the assorted evils of two lessers. The problem is compounded by a very simple fact: there are no betters than these two lessers. No third party is or will ever be viable. The deck is stacked against them.

Contrary to what we may say and the polemical frustration conservatives too often are forced to express about the Republican Party, there remain very real differences between the two parties—life and death differences that cannot be underestimated or ignored.

It is easy to say both parties are appalling. They are. It becomes very difficult to figure out what to do about it. There is, however, a starting point. As bad as you or I may think the Republican Party has been at times, at least it will not sell us down the river to our nation's enemies. At least it will more often than not support businesses and individuals against the government. At least it will support you working for yourself over you working to give money to someone else.

Despite the real differences, too often Republican leaders prefer to find ever-shrinking common ground with the Left rather than make a stand on opposing ground fighting for free people and free markets against the leviathan of government. With the rise of the tea party movement, conservatives must unite to clean up the Republican Party. If they don't, voters will keep rejecting Republican pseudo-socialists in favor of authentic socialists.

With the starting point being to clean house within the GOP, the next question is how. To figure out how, we must examine the past as the path to the present. Both parties have used the tax code, spending, and power to reward their bases, enact their preferred social policies, and expand their own preferred government programs.

Politicians of both parties have gone to Washington not to reduce its size, but expand what it can do for preferred interest groups. Some conservatives have become devoid of ideas other than the acquisition of power. The GOP started making shortcut calculations like big business = good, instead of entrepreneurs = good. There is a difference; but too many have grown too complacent to see it.

Enough is enough.

With the rise of the tea party movement, America has a chance of turning back from its current path to poverty. But tea party activists need to realize something along the way. While we refer herein to "tea partiers," the fact is the tea party movement's branding could use a bit of work.

I don't know about you, but when I hear tea partiers talk about the issues they care about, I think they are American issues, not tea party issues. Segregating them into something other than American issues is a dangerous game. With the way the media works, it becomes easier to paint tea partiers as fringe when in fact the issues they care about are very American. While we may refer to each other as tea partiers, we need to be very careful and understand that our issues are American issues. They are not subject to segregation from normal political discourse.

The ideas we pursue to solve our issues are not subject to segregation into some sort of subset of conservatism. They are not paleo-conservative, neo-conservative, or any sort of hyphenated conservatism. The ideas are conservative. And they are ideas worth fighting for in a country where a majority leans right-of-center, and people understand intrinsically if government would just get out of the way, we could thrive.

That's the reality of our situation. You can choose to get involved and fight for freedom, or you can sit on the sidelines. But let me tell you, while you decide to do nothing, the other side intends to change your way of life. They have chosen to do something and the change they want to bring is not change any free person should want.

So you have a choice: get involved or not.

Ronald Reagan said freedom is only one generation away from ending. Let us not allow it to end in this generation.

People remember Paul Revere. Few people remember Dr. Samuel Prescott. At 1:00 a.m. on April 19, 1775, Revere ran into Prescott, who was on his way home from a party. Prescott was willing to help. Without Prescott's knowledge of the farms surrounding them, Revere's task would have been all the more difficult that night. And when Revere rode out into the countryside, Prescott stayed behind on the farms and in his town rallying people, and got his brother to go to the next town to rally people. They were not Paul Revere, but they joined him and added to his voice. Revere could not have gotten the job done without them.

We cannot get the job done without each other. It is time to unite. And it is time to fight. Together, Freedom will prevail. But to begin the fight, we must educate ourselves on why we fight. We must be sure of what we believe.

"DON'T TREAD ON ME"

I n 2005, conservatives saw George W. Bush nominate Harriet Miers to the United States Supreme Court. Within minutes of her appointment, we noted at RedState.com that Miers had given a campaign donation to Al Gore in 1988. Despite George W. Bush's steel tariffs, the No Child Left Behind Act, and the Medicare Part D expansion, conservatives had begrudgingly stuck with him. He kept us safe and was better than the other guy. The Miers nomination became the first visible break between conservatives and Republicans.

The Miers nomination debacle was followed by George Bush's comprehensive immigration plan. Emboldened by the withdrawal of Harriet Miers' nomination, conservatives united in opposition and won. In 2008, bank bailouts and the General Motors fiasco caused conservatives to yet again split not just from George W. Bush, but from the Republican Party. A rift was created that remains unrepaired.

In 2009, as the citizens of the United States were getting fed up with Washington's bailouts and arrogance, they started rallying together at tax time and during town hall meetings. A little yellow flag popped up with increasing frequency, emblazoned with a simple but powerful message for those in power: "Don't Tread on Me." Luckily for George W. Bush, what happened next became Barack Obama's problem.

Many Americans who had never been politically active, never walked a precinct, never interrupted their golf games, family gatherings, or vacations to discuss politics, government, or the Constitution, were suddenly gripped with the sense that their government, nation, and way of life were being stolen from them. Average Americans began stepping out of their homes, shops, and RVs to declare that their America was threatened, and they were going to defend her. They proclaimed themselves members of a new "Tea Party" in honor of the defiant patriots who dumped British tea into the Boston Harbor. Free people in danger of losing their freedom are a force to be reckoned with.

It may not have been any one action of newly elected President Barack Obama or his cohorts in destroying America—Senator Reid and Speaker Pelosi—that precipitated the revolt of individual Americans. It was a combination of words, positions, comments, attitudes, facial expressions, body language, speeches, votes, and other signals that prompted Americans to get out of their easy chairs to march on Washington. Its origins were seeded by Republicans who lost their way. Democrats intent on exploiting our troubles, however, are reaping the harvest of discontent.

There have been so many reasons to become alarmed about America's future and that of our children and grandchildren. Consider just a few domestic issues:

ObamaCare was crammed down the throats of Americans against their collective will with lies, threats, and phony accounting numbers, and only after corrupting the legislative process and resorting to an unconstitutional mandate to purchase health insurance. Despite promises of transparency and full debate on the bill, only insiders saw it, and no legislator read it. It was a total desecration of the legislative process.

Freedom of speech and our conservative talk radio and television hosts are threatened by the Obama Administration's reactivation of the so-called "fairness doctrine."

Global warming mythology, rather than science, underpins the continued effort to reduce CO_2 emissions (greenhouse gases) which will destroy jobs and drive electric and heating bills through the roof.

Obama continues to press for card-check legislation to aid his union backers by eliminating secret ballots for workers in union elections.

The Welfare Reform Act (signed by Bill Clinton in 1996) has been gutted by Obama's regulations and executive orders, despite its success in significantly cutting costs along with the number of those on welfare. Obama has once again paid off his public-employee union allies by creating many new union-dues-paying jobs, fueling old-style welfare costs as people grow more dependent on government not just for handouts, but for their employment.

Bailouts of Obama's Wall Street friends and takeover of major industries has put the American taxpayer at increasing risk and generated unprecedented future liabilities and unfunded obligations. What began under George W. Bush has mushroomed.

The recession has been worsened by Obama's preoccupation with radical new domestic policies, taxes, and expenditures—alarming, rather than calming, potential job-creators.

The Democrats' embrace of "too big to fail" perpetuates the moral hazard of risky financial schemes inundating taxpayers while rewarding lobbyists and other special interests with the power to choose the winners and the losers among competing businesses.

On the national defense, foreign policy, and international security front, Obama continues to denigrate our nation, undermine our allies, and put our national interests at risk. Consider:

Missile-defense systems in Poland and the Czech Republic were unilaterally cut by Obama, badly undercutting defense of Western Europe.

The North Korea missile firings in 2009 and the torpedoing of a South Korean naval vessel in 2010 produced no U.S. response.

Iran's pursuit of nuclear-weapons, and its systematic abuse of its freedom-seeking citizens, have been met with Obama's silence.

The bilateral nuclear disarmament treaty with Russia is fraught with danger and is likely to be rejected by the United States Senate. At a time when Barack Obama is playing nice with the Russians, the FBI is rounding up spies deeply embedded within American industry. There is no guarantee Russia will honor the treaty.

Relations with Great Britain, France, and Germany are regressing.

In Central America's Honduras, Obama backed the defrocked leader who partnered with our enemies Hugo Chavez and Fidel Castro. Obama did so in the face of the Honduran Supreme Court's decision that to allow the president to continue in office would be unconstitutional.[1]

China continues to make inroads in South American countries as the United States fails to develop a foreign policy strategy to support freedom in South and Central American countries.

Meanwhile, Obama continues to make statements and take actions alien to the interests of the United States and that denigrate our honor and history:

He continues to apologize for America as if we didn't save the world from the Axis in World War II and the Soviets in the Cold War.

He failed to go to Berlin to honor the fall of the Berlin Wall and America's role in the collapse of communism.

Ignoring our roots, founding, and traditions, he has said the United States is not a Christian nation.

He antagonizes Israel and slights its elected leaders in their efforts to contain Islamic terrorism.

He uses rhetoric for job creators and Wall Street that would be better reserved for Al Qaeda.

He sues Arizona to stop the state from enforcing existing immigration law while shutting down American parkland because it is too dangerous for American citizens.[2]

As tea partiers witness the Washington attacks on American values and the shredding of the Constitution and the Bill of Rights, is it any wonder they feel like slaves rather than masters of their government?

Making matters worse, the Republicans in Washington have refused to change. The political courage the Republican leadership is showing is manifested in the Senate Republicans rejecting conservative candidates across the nation in favor of milquetoast moderates or liberals while the House Republicans are trying with all their might to stop a conservative-led effort to repeal ObamaCare and start over.

For good reason the tea parties—the American public—have resurrected "Don't Tread on Me." More specifically, conservatives are finally intent on taking back the Republican Party from establishment forces that seek to win at any cost, damn the ideas.

With great pride and determination, Americans are ready to fight to take back their country. That is the silver lining of the storm clouds threatening America's future.

CHAPTER 1

REPUBLICANS IN CHARGE: PRO-LIFE STATISTS

In this present crisis, government is not the solution to our problem; government is the problem. From time to time we've been tempted to believe that society has become too complex to be managed by self-rule, that government by an elite group is superior to govern-ment for, by, and of the people. Well, if no one among us is capable of governing himself, then who among us has the capacity to govern someone else? All of us together, in and out of government, must bear the burden. The solutions we seek must be equitable, with no one group singled out to pay a higher price.[1]

—PRESIDENT RONALD W. REAGAN, FIRST INAUGURAL ADDRESS,
JANUARY 20, 1981

Most people endeavoring to write a book like this would immediately start with the Obama Administration and how the Democrats have worked to destroy the country. Intellectual integrity, however, requires that the beginning be with the Republicans.

Many conservatives feel the Republican Party is as bad as the Dem-ocratic Party. Though Republican leaders have collaborated with the Democrats to grow government for their own ends, on issues from the sanctity of life to national security, there are overwhelming life and death differences. Nonetheless, the Republicans lost their way during the administration of George W. Bush. Sadly, too many conservatives were corrupted along the way. The only way to fix the problem is to honestly examine it, so we don't repeat our mistakes.

The starting point for this discussion has a specific date: August 15, 2003. On that day, Fred Barnes of the *Weekly Standard* wrote a now infamous op-ed in the *Wall Street Journal* in defense of George W. Bush's administration. That op-ed coined the phrase "big government conservative."

IS PRESIDENT BUSH really a conservative? When that question came up this summer, the White House went into crisis mode. Bush aides summoned several of Washington's conservative journalists to a 6:30 a.m. breakfast at the White House to press the case for the president's adherence to conservative principles. Aides outnumbered journalists. Other conservative writers and broadcasters were invited to luncheon sessions. They heard a similar spiel.

The White House needn't have bothered. The case for Bush's conservatism is strong. Sure, some conservatives are upset because he has tolerated a surge in federal spending, downplayed swollen deficits, failed to use his veto, created a vast Department of Homeland Security, and fashioned an alliance of sorts with Teddy Kennedy on education and Medicare. But the real gripe is that Bush isn't their kind of conventional conservative. Rather, he's a big government conservative. This isn't a description he or other prominent conservatives willingly embrace. It makes them sound as if they aren't conservatives at all. But they are. They simply believe in using what would normally be seen as liberal means— activist government—for conservative ends. And they're willing to spend more and increase the size of government in the process.

Being a big government conservative doesn't bring Bush close to being a moderate, much less a liberal. On most issues, his position is standard conservative: a pro-lifer who expects to sign a ban on partial birth abortion, he's against stem-cell research and gun control, and has drawn the line at gay marriage. His judicial nominees are so uniformly conservative that liberals are furious.[2]

It is a failing of many on the Right to claim that those who support tax cuts and oppose abortion are conservative. Conservatism must go beyond that. As Ronald Reagan said, "Government is not the solution to our problem; government is the problem." That was true in 1981. That was true in 2003. It is true today.

Fast forward from Fred Barnes' August 15, 2003 op-ed, to August 15, 2005, and this *Washington Post* editorial entitled "Big Government Conservatives":

Back in 1987, when Mr. Reagan applied his veto to what was generally known at the time as the highway and mass transit bill, he was offended by the 152 earmarks for pet projects favored by members of Congress. But on Wednesday Mr. Bush signed a transportation bill containing no fewer than 6,371 earmarks. Each one of these, as Mr. Reagan understood but Mr. Bush apparently doesn't, amounts to a conscious decision to waste taxpayers' dollars. One point of an earmark is to direct money to a project that would not receive money as a result of rational judgments based on cost-benefit analyses.

Mr. Bush, who had threatened to veto wasteful spending bills, chose instead to cave in. He did so despite the fact that in addition to a record number of earmarks the transportation bill came with a price tag that he had once called unacceptable. The bill has a declared cost of $286 billion over five years plus a concealed cost of a further $9 billion; Mr. Bush had earlier drawn a line in the sand at $256 billion, then drawn another line at $284 billion. Asked to explain the president's capitulation, a White House spokesman pleaded that at least this law would be less costly than the 2003 Medicare reform. This is a classic case of defining deviancy down.[3]

Conservatives must be willing to accept that being pro-life and pro-tax cuts does not a conservative make. In most every way, Republicans, particularly the leadership of the Republican Party, have behaved as pro-life statists—big government guys who are socially conservative and fiscally reckless.

If the Republican Party is willing to expand government for allegedly conservative ends, the Democrats have a free pass to do the same for liberal ends. Unless the Republican Party is willing to be the party of individual choice, the party of entrepreneurs—the party of conservatives—we will not beat back the leviathan of government.

But let us not kid ourselves. The Republican Party did not actually use government for purely "conservative ends." It is not the Second Amendment vote or the pro-life vote that count. Those votes are popular with a majority of Americans. The votes that count are those taken in committee or behind the scenes or even on the floor of Congress expanding government programs, regulation, and encroachment on free markets and free people. Time and again, the Republican majority did just that.

In fact, that is perhaps the greatest sin in the Republican Party. With exceptions like Mike Pence and Jim DeMint, too few Republican were ever willing to stand up for conservatism against statism when the Republicans were in charge. Steel tariffs, imposed by President Bush in 2002, were just the beginning of the increase in government that came to define Republicans' time in power.

FAILING TO KEEP THE SPIRIT OF '94

In 1994, the Republican Party took back control of both houses of Congress for the first time in forty years. In doing so, they presented the American public with a document entitled the "Contract With America."

The Contract had eight reforms it sought to accomplish with ten pieces of legislation and changes to rules in the House of Representatives.[4] The reforms were designed to:

- require all laws that apply to the rest of the country also apply equally to the Congress;
- select a major, independent auditing firm to conduct a comprehensive audit of Congress for waste, fraud or abuse;
- cut the number of House committees, and cut committee staff by one-third;
- limit the terms of all committee chairs;
- ban the casting of proxy votes in committee;
- require committee meetings to be open to the public;
- require a three-fifths majority vote to pass a tax increase;
- guarantee an honest accounting of our Federal Budget by implementing zero base-line budgeting.

The ten pieces of legislation[5] were:

- THE FISCAL RESPONSIBILITY ACT: A balanced budget/tax limitation amendment and a legislative line-item veto to restore fiscal responsibility to an out-of-control Congress, requiring them to live under the same budget constraints as families and businesses.
- THE TAKING BACK OUR STREETS ACT: An anti-crime package including stronger truth-in-sentencing, "good faith" exclusionary rule exemptions, effective death penalty

provisions, and cuts in social spending from [a 1994] crime bill to fund prison construction and additional law enforcement to keep people secure in their neighborhoods and kids safe in their schools.

■ THE PERSONAL RESPONSIBILITY ACT: Discourage illegitimacy and teen pregnancy by prohibiting welfare to minor mothers and denying increased AFDC [Aid to Families with Dependent Children; i.e., welfare] for additional children while on welfare, cut spending for welfare programs, and enact a tough two-years-and-out provision with work requirements to promote individual responsibility.

■ THE FAMILY REINFORCEMENT ACT: Child support enforcement, tax incentives for adoption, strengthening rights of parents in their children's education, stronger child pornography laws, and an elderly dependent care tax credit to reinforce the central role of families in American society.

■ THE AMERICAN DREAM RESTORATION ACT: A $500 per child tax credit, begin repeal of the marriage tax penalty, and creation of American Dream Savings Accounts to provide middle-class tax relief.

■ THE NATIONAL SECURITY RESTORATION ACT: No U.S. troops under UN command and restoration of the essential parts of our national security funding to strengthen our national defense and maintain our credibility around the world.

■ THE SENIOR CITIZENS FAIRNESS ACT: Raise the Social Security earnings limit which currently forces seniors out of the work force, repeal the 1993 tax hikes on Social Security benefits, and provide tax incentives for private long-term care insurance to let older Americans keep more of what they have earned over the years.

- THE JOB CREATION AND WAGE ENHANCEMENT ACT: Small business incentives, capital gains cut and indexation, neutral cost recovery, risk assessment/cost-benefit analysis, strengthening the Regulatory Flexibility Act and unfunded mandate reform to create jobs and raise worker wages.
- THE COMMON SENSE LEGAL REFORM ACT: "Loser pays" laws, reasonable limits on punitive damages, and reform of product liability laws to stem the endless tide of litigation.
- THE CITIZEN LEGISLATURE ACT: A first-ever vote on term limits to replace career politicians with citizen legislators.

The Contract only promised that the legislation would go to the floor of the House of Representatives for debate. Some of the measures passed. Some did not. Edward H. Crane, the founder and president of the CATO Institute, wrote in *Forbes Magazine* on November 13, 2000,

> Over the past three years the Republican-controlled Congress has approved discretionary spending that exceeded Bill Clinton's requests by more than $30 billion. The party that in 1994 would abolish the Department of Education now brags in response to Clinton's 2000 State of the Union Address that it is outspending the White House when it comes to education. My colleagues Stephen Moore and Stephen Slivinski found that *the combined budgets of the 95 major programs that the Contract with America promised to eliminate have increased by 13%*. Republican congressional candidates are frightened to be associated with George W. Bush's sensible proposal to allow Americans to invest a portion of their Social Security taxes in real assets.[6] (Emphasis added)

My, how far the Republicans have drifted. A Balanced Budget Amendment is nowhere to be found. Republicans have presided over massive growth in government. More and more politicians have become a professional class of political elites and show regular disdain for the average person—let alone conservatives. Consider the implications of that professional class of political elites.

A July 23, 2010 Rasmussen survey found "75% of Likely Voters prefer free markets over a government managed economy. Just 14% think a government managed economy is better while 11% are not sure." But, among those considered the political class, which transcends party lines, "a government managed economy [is preferred] over free markets by a 44% to 37% margin. . . . [A]mong Mainstream voters, 90% prefer the free market. Outside of the Political Class, free markets are preferred across all demographic and partisan lines."[7]

Republican leaders in Washington, like their Democratic colleagues, have developed a profound sense of their own righteousness and infallibility, both of which are at odds with history and the opinions of the American public.

Observe, for example, former Senate Majority Leader Trent Lott (R-MS), who is now a lobbyist in Washington. The *Washington Post* contained this nugget in the run-up to the 2010 elections:

> Former Senate majority leader Trent Lott (R-Miss.), now a D.C. lobbyist, warned that a robust bloc of rabble-rousers spells further Senate dysfunction. "We don't need a lot of Jim DeMint disciples," Lott said in an interview. "As soon as they get here, we need to co-opt them."
>
> But Lott said he's not expecting a tea-party sweep. "I still have faith in the visceral judgment of the American people," he said.[8]

Lott's contempt was shared in the article by Senator Robert Bennett (R-UT), whom tea party activists defeated in his re-election effort. Behind the scenes, the leadership of the Republican Party has been openly contemptuous of the tea party movement. The Senate Republican Leader, Mitch McConnell, ran his 2008 re-election campaign in Kentucky on the pork he brought into the state. In 2010, he opposed his conservative Kentucky colleague Jim Bunning's re-election efforts, which in part led to Bunning dropping out.

McConnell worked with Senator Harry Reid to keep the push for the Troubled Asset Relief Program (TARP) alive despite it being deeply unpopular with conservatives.[9] In 1994, Washington Republicans decided to put the country first. Ever since, they've been putting Washington first. That has led to an enormous growth of government.

The National Senatorial Campaign Committee (NRSC), the body charged with electing Republicans to Congress, made a conscious decision in the 2010 election to recruit moderates. In Florida, the Republicans recruited the liberal Republican Governor Charlie Crist, while conservatives rallied to Marco Rubio. Crist, unable to win, left the Republican Party to challenge Rubio from the left as an independent.

In Pennsylvania, the NRSC stood with Arlen Specter against former Congressman Pat Toomey. When Senator Jim DeMint stood up and declared his support for Toomey, Specter became a Democrat. In Colorado, national Republicans embraced former Colorado Lieutenant Governor Jane Norton against Colorado District Attorney Ken Buck, whom Jim DeMint supported.

NRSC Chairman Senator John Cornyn told the *Washington Post*, "The candidates are not ours to choose. They're the choice of the primary voters in the states, and I think we should respect their choices."[10] This, after Cornyn had endorsed Charlie Crist in Florida and gone fundraising for Jane Norton in Colorado.

In New York, the Republican establishment lined up behind Dede Scozzafava, a liberal Republican and union sympathizer. Conservatives rallied and drove her from the race, but their third party candidate in 2009, Doug Hoffman, running under the Conservative Party's banner, lost to Democrat Bill Owens, whose positions in the campaign were to the right of the Republican. Time and again, when given the opportunity, the Republican establishment endorsed liberals and moderates, while impugning or opposing conservatives who ran with the Spirit of '94 in their campaigns.

FAILURE TO HOLD EACH OTHER ACCOUNTABLE

It is not easy, but it is necessary to hold one's own party accountable—sometimes publicly. It is better when the politicians themselves do it. In 1994, the Republicans scored such a massive victory, many people went to Congress who probably should not have. Others who had been there for a while were emboldened to head off toward corruption.

Duke Cunningham is but one example. Cunningham went to jail after receiving kickbacks from a defense contractor. But his story is one among many. The federal government indicted Congressman Rick Renzi (R-AZ) in 2008 over a land deal.[11] Congressman Robert Ney (R-OH) pled guilty to corruption charges related to the Jack Abramoff scandal and, while in office, spent a month in treatment for alcoholism.[12] Representative Mark Foley resigned in 2006 after it emerged that he sent sexually explicit messages to a House page.[13]

Then there are the adultery issues of Republicans in Congress. Jesus Christ may have said, "Judge not lest you be judged,"[14] but Republicans should at least live by a higher standard than Democrats. Either that, or they need to do as good a job as the Democrats in not getting caught.

This matters, because as Alexis De Tocqueville said, "Liberty cannot be established without morality, nor morality without faith."[15] Conservatives understand true liberty requires morality. Conservatives should not settle for "everybody else does it." This does not mean conservatives should seek to impose their morality on others, but it does mean they should be governed by a moral code when governing others.

Republicans must hold themselves accountable. Failing to hold themselves accountable leaves that accountability with the voters. And the voters are not afraid to throw the bums out.

EXPANDING THE STATE

Under the Republicans, the nation saw government explode with the Medicare Prescription Drug Benefit and No Child Left Behind. George W. Bush largely let the late senator Ted Kennedy draft No Child Left Behind. Republicans touted school choice provisions in it, which amounted to finding a pearl after shucking a million rotten oysters. The Republicans also created "Faith-Based Initiatives," which sounded good, but which conservatives should have shied away from because of the dangerous and very real potential for government encroachment on the free exercise of religion.

Republican actions during the beginning of the twenty-first century did not just increase spending. Their actions took away freedom and betrayed the very real sense of the GOP being for entrepreneurs and individuals. In effect, the GOP decided to run as Democrat-Lite. Unfortunately, while the Democrats seem to have recognized in 2010 with the passage of ObamaCare that there is no such thing as a permanent political majority, but a permanent policy victory is possible, the Republican Party continues to run in search of a permanent majority, refusing to fight necessary fights for smaller government along the way.

Contrary to popular belief, it was not the Obama Administration that gave us the Troubled Asset Relief Program ("TARP"), but George W. Bush. In a CNN interview, President Bush declared, "I've abandoned free-market principles to save the free-market system."[16] Really?

At first, Republicans in Congress blocked the initial push to pass TARP. At a press conference following its initial defeat, House Minority Whip Eric Cantor (R-VA) stood up with the transcript of Nancy Pelosi's speech on the floor of the House of Representatives, blasting the Republicans for the economic collapse. Cantor said Republicans voted against TARP because Nancy Pelosi had not been nice to them. Really?

Senate Republican Leader Mitch McConnell took to the floor of the Senate and said of the Senate vote on TARP, "I think this is one of the finest moments in the history of the Senate."[17] Really?

Inevitably, most Republicans caved to White House and Congressional leadership pressure and voted in favor of the Troubled Asset Relief Program.

The GOP wasn't done there. George Bush also pushed through the auto bailout with the aid of some Republicans. Both TARP and the auto bailout created the idea that some companies are "too big to fail." Doing so put big businesses in a better position than small businesses, setting up legal parameters by which big businesses could behave in riskier ways than entrepreneurs, knowing the government would bail them out.

No one should have been surprised by the GOP's conduct. Again and again, the Republican Party played to type as the party of big oil/ pharma/banks/business/tobacco, all while ignoring the entrepreneurial class. That's okay though—the GOP had the Bush tax cuts. For some reason, the Republicans felt that absolved them of all sins. It did not.

George W. Bush championed the idea of an ownership society. The idea among conservatives, which remains in things like Congressman Paul Ryan's Roadmap (explored in more detail in Chapter 9), was that once Americans are given control over their destiny, it will be tough for government to take it back. On June 17, 2004, the president started off his pitch with "[I]f you own something, you have a vital stake in the future of our country. The more ownership there is in

America, the more vitality there is in America, and the more people have a vital stake in the future of this country."[18] The White House released a fact sheet with a summary reading, "American families should have choices and access they need to affordable healthcare and homeownership; Americans should have the option of managing their own retirement; and small businesses, which employ over half of all workers, need lower taxes and fewer government mandates so they can grow."[19]

At a speech to the National Association of Home Builders on October 2, 2004, President Bush said, "We're creating...an ownership society in this country, where more Americans than ever will be able to open up their door where they live and say, welcome to my house, welcome to my piece of property."[20]

This theme echoed his acceptance speech at the Republican National Convention in New York a month earlier on September 2, 2004. "Another priority for a new term is to build an ownership society, because ownership brings security and dignity and independence," he said.[21]

But what the Republicans actually did looked nothing like an ownership society. In fact, the GOP caved quickly on social security reform, despite Bush's push for it in his second term, refusing to give individuals the option of a private account. The GOP failures went beyond that. Republicans made it more expensive for entrepreneurs and individuals to live.

In typical fashion, with the meltdown of Enron, Worldcom, and other big companies in the early part of the 2000's, Congress, both Republicans and Democrats, decided new laws were needed, even though the companies were violating existing laws. Thus, in bipartisan destructive fashion, the GOP cooperated with the Democrats to pass the Sarbanes-Oxley Act.[22] *Forbes* claimed, "Sarbanes-Oxley is consistently called the broadest-sweeping legislation to affect corporations and public accounting since the 1933 and 1934 securities acts."[23] Michael Malone, writing in the *Wall Street Journal,* noted,

According to the National Venture Capital Association, in all of 2008 there have been just six companies that have gone public. Compare that with 269 IPOs in 1999, 272 in 1996, and 365 in 1986....For all of this, we can first thank Sarbanes-Oxley. Cooked up in the wake of accounting scandals earlier this decade, it has essentially killed the creation of new public companies in America, hamstrung the NYSE and Nasdaq (while making the London Stock Exchange rich), and cost U.S. industry more than $200 billion by some estimates.[24]

In fact, more and more evidence suggests Sarbanes-Oxley not only drove up the costs of doing business for American businesses, particularly small businesses on the verge of going public, but also chased a lot of capital and initial public offerings overseas to London. A presentation of the International Business Law Committee of the American Bar Association, found "From 1996–2002, [the New York Stock Exchange] averaged 51 international listings per year. From 2003–2006, that average declined to 21. In 2006, only two of the 25 largest IPOs in the world chose to register and list in the United States; both are domestic companies."[25]

Time and again, Republicans have abandoned free market principles when the heat is on and have opted for more government, not less. Doing so keeps driving up the tax bill as well as the costs of doing business.

Even in energy and farming, Republicans abandon the free market. Republicans had the chance and refused to back away from corn-based ethanol production. The Energy Policy Act of 2005 mandated 7.5 billion gallons of ethanol production a year.[26] The mandate for ethanol, naturally, drove up food prices. Bloomberg reported on November 22, 2006, "Global ethanol production is driving up prices for food commodities, from feed stocks such as sugar, to meat, said Datagro, Brazil's biggest sugar-industry forecasting firm. U.S. production, forecast to increase more than 70 percent by 2012, will use 37 percent of the country's current corn supply to meet output needs, up 15 percent from 2006, Datagro said."[27]

In 2007, with Democrats in charge of Congress, the ethanol mandate became 15 billion gallons. No believer in free markets would ever accept that mandates do any good. In fact, the editors of *National Review* found it did quite a bit of harm.

> As farmers grow more corn in hopes of selling it to ethanol makers, they also threaten to disrupt the water supply in some regions. That's because farmers are both planting new corn on formerly uncultivated soil, and converting acres already under cultivation toward corn and away from other, less water-intensive food crops. To put the current expansion of corn production into perspective, consider that we have more corn growing on American soil right now than at any time since World War II, when the farms of Europe had been devastated by war and America was feeding two continents.[28]

Naturally, with the start of the 2008 Presidential season, Republicans fell all over themselves to worship at the feet of Iowa corn farmers.

The Republicans also never reined in farm subsidies for giant corporations. Despite their ethanol policies driving up the cost of corn, their sugar tariffs driving up the cost of sugar, and their allowing federal price regulations on milk to continue after the expiration of the Northeast Interstate Dairy Compact, the GOP also kept farm subsidies in place. The Republicans even went so far as to eradicate the free market reforms put into place in the Freedom to Farm Act of 1996 through their various farm bills during George W. Bush's administration.[29]

Then there are earmarks and spending. The Republicans championed the Gravina Island Bridge earmark in Alaska, which famously became known as the "Bridge to Nowhere."[30] The moniker stuck, and soon Republicans were left to defend "railroads to nowhere" and "roads to nowhere." A grassroots movement called "Porkbusters" sprung up to oppose earmarks, prompting former Senate Republican Leader Trent Lott to declare, "I'll just say this about the so-called porkbusters. I'm getting damn tired of hearing from them. They have been nothing but trouble ever since Katrina."[31]

The fight over earmarks was one of the biggest between the Republican Party and conservative grassroots during the Bush Administration. While conservatives, for a long time, kept quiet because George W. Bush kept the country safe during war, conservatives recognized their silence came with a price. They ceded the moral high ground on spending, allowing Democrats to get their foot in the door and claim to be more responsible. It took Barack Obama to prove that a lie, but the damage was done.

In the past decade, it has been far more likely for the Republican Party to compromise in favor of big government than for the Democratic Party to compromise in favor of the free markets. That must change. Part of that change must come from Republican voters throwing out Republicans who go, in Margaret Thatcher's words, "wobbly."[32] In that equation, Republicans must recognize that not all conservatives are created equal.

EARMARXISTS

Every election year, conservatives are faced with the same dilemma—wondering whether a Republican politician who claims to be a conservative is the real deal or the type who goes along to get along and will end up being part of the problem.

For self-described conservatives, it is easy to be pro-life, pro-troops, and pro-tax cuts. In most races, that is not how you separate the wheat from the chaff. You separate them on the basis of their belief in limited government. And there is no better bellwether of politician's pro-clivities toward limited government than whether they request and defend earmarks.

Many defenders of the Republican establishment don't want to talk about earmarks. *Earmarks are not the problem!* they say. *They amount to such a small portion of the federal budget. Earmarks are the only way to deal with an intransigent bureaucracy. They divide Republicans when we should be focused on battling the Obama Administration's liberal agenda. Earmarks are the only form of constitutional spending and need to be defended no matter how unpopular. It's about the CONSTITUTION—didn't you know??*

The arguments are many, but they are all full of holes.

Yes, earmarks amount to a small percentage of the budget, and compared to the enormity of the entitlement crisis of Social Security, Medicare, and Medicaid, they are miniscule. But as Jeff Flake and Tom Coburn have said before, earmarks are the gateway drug to higher spending. If a politician thinks his reelection bid is in jeopardy because he won't be able to deliver a bike path or high-speed rail project to his district, it is inconceivable to think that that same politician will sign up for allowing people to redirect their FICA taxes to personal accounts or slow the growth of Medicare. Earmarks erode the ability to say no to more government, and they corrupt often-good politicians with the enjoyment and the power of directing other people's money to those who come to them and ask. And at times, earmarks directly enable increased government when they are used to buy lawmakers off. It is standard procedure for powerful Chairmen to demand that anyone with earmarks in a bill vote for the overall bill lest the projects get struck. Look no further than the Cornhusker Kickback and the Louisiana Purchase, used to pass ObamaCare in the Senate.

Yes, earmarks afford lawmakers an avenue to keep some nameless bureaucrat from sending all the federal dollars somewhere else, but then why are you so set on federal dollars flowing to your district?

If you believe in limited government, why do you want your district to get its "fair share"? Let's take the most conservative of earmarks—highway projects, like a vital bridge or intersection that will alleviate traffic. Never mind that the federal interstate system has long been built, meaning highway funding could be devolved to the states so that the vast majority of districts are not donor districts, meaning they contribute more in gas taxes than they get back. The whole point of the highway program is now to earmark and to give federal lawmakers power to direct taxpayer dollars.[33] But do you think this sort of federalist argument would be made by an earmarxist? No, they would be spending their political capital getting theirs too.

Congress does have the power to spend money, but the vast majority of earmarks are spent on completely unconstitutional projects and activities.

Yes, earmarks are "divisive," and making them an issue is bound to put many Republicans in a difficult spot. That should not be a conservative's concern. After all the attention paid to earmarks over the last few years, if politicians are still earmarking—no matter how "transparent" (the ready-made reform for any earmarxist)—they can't say they were not forewarned. In fact, they very likely think they can get away with it. A Republican Congress isn't worth having if it is not going to be a conservative one, filled with men and women who believe in limited government, and who can say no to those who come to the federal government asking for more. Do we really want to spend all this time and effort working to get so-called conservatives elected who will fail us yet again?

Of course not. So let me say it. Earmarks are certainly not the only issue, but they are the most telling as to whether Republicans really have learned their lesson in the minority.

- Criticize any "agenda" or any "contract" from any Republican leader or Republican entity which doesn't include an immediate, unilateral earmark moratorium.
- Do not accept the conservative bona fides of any politician who has failed to adopt an earmark moratorium or who argues for them.
- Do not allow any politician to speak to a tea party rally unless he or she has taken a pledge not to request earmarks.

Earmarks have become one of the chief vehicles for the Republican expansion of government. It is time to purge the earmarxists from the conservative movement and Republican leadership.

FOREIGN POLICY

Republicans and conservatives have failed, in the past decade, to develop a common and shared framework for foreign policy, and we will not endeavor to wade into the various policy positions. But, it should be said that Republicans in the Bush years failed miserably to expand freedom in South America, leaving at least eleven countries receiving military training from China instead of the United States.[34]

In North Korea, George W. Bush's administration accepted 5-way talks with lots of broken promises by North Korea and no enforcement mechanisms for the United States. Iran has continued its nuclear program. Republicans continued to buy into the ridiculous notion of a "two-state" solution between Israel and those who want to see it wiped off the map.

While many times better than the Democrats on issues of war and foreign affairs, we should not delude ourselves into thinking Republicans have been perfect. The Republican failure to deal with the growing threat from China during the Bush years will haunt us for a long while.

FAILING TO FIGHT FOR FREEDOM

In *The Gathering Storm*, Sir Winston Churchill summed up the necessary fight for freedom:

> If you will not fight for the right when you can easily win without bloodshed, if you will not fight when your victory will be sure and not too costly, you may come to the moment when you will have to fight with all the odds against you and only a small chance of survival. There may even be a worse case: you may have to fight when there is no hope of victory, because it is better to perish than to live as slaves.[35]

Conservatives have a profound belief that the fight for freedom is necessary. That fight may not be on the battlefield, but it is a fight nonetheless. Unfortunately, sometimes well-meaning Republicans go to Washington, get co-opted, and abandon the idea of federalism. In a nutshell, Republicans too often get to Washington and believe Washington can solve all our ills. Washington cannot.

Conservatives sometimes even go to Washington and forget the states were the originators of the federal government, and the federal constitution gives Congress only limited powers. Consider Utah Senator Robert Bennett, defeated in 2010 by conservative activists because he went to Washington and lost his way.

Many Washington conservatives scratched their heads, perplexed that conservative activists would seek to oust such an allegedly dependable conservative. Bennett, however, was like too many of his colleagues, another big government statist who happened to support tax cuts and was pro-life.

On Christmas Eve 2009, the Senate of the United States voted on a constitutional point of order raised by Senators Jim DeMint and John Ensign. The Senators challenged the constitutionality of the individual mandate in the Democrats' healthcare legislation. The individual mandate is a federally imposed requirement that every man, woman, and child in the United States obtain health insurance on pain of financial penalty or, in the Democrats' proposal at the time, jail.

Put more plainly, if you choose not to have health insurance, the Congress of the United States intends to punish you by taking away your property or your life via incarceration.

All thirty-nine of the Republican senators still present in Washington voted that it is unconstitutional to impose an individual mandate on the citizens of the United States.[36]

But Bob Bennett, Lamar Alexander, Mike Crapo, Lindsey Graham, and Judd Gregg are all co-sponsors of S.391, the Wyden-Bennett healthcare plan. The legislation, named for its chief sponsors Ron Wyden (D-OR) and Bob Bennett (R-UT), imposes an individual mandate on American citizens. Section 102 of the legislation is entitled "Individual Responsibility to Enroll in a Healthy Americans Private Insurance Plan."[37] The section outlines how the feds will punish you if you refuse to buy an insurance plan.

In fact, that is precisely what Bennett, Alexander, Crapo, Graham, and Gregg claimed was unconstitutional. Republican senators who would vote that something is unconstitutional while co-sponsoring legislation doing the that very thing is the epitome of what conservatives must fight against inside the Republican Party.

After passage of ObamaCare, Republicans refused an all-out fight to repeal it. In fact, most Republican leaders claimed that in order to repeal "ObamaCare" Republicans would have to offer something equally comprehensive.[38] When Representative Steve King (R-IA) launched a discharge petition[39] on legislation to repeal ObamaCare, House Republican leaders John Boehner and Eric Cantor decided to muddy the water by offering up a second discharge petition from Representative Wally Herger (R-TX) that repealed ObamaCare and replaced it with something else. The strategy gave Blue Dog Democrats who had been on the campaign trail saying they would vote against ObamaCare if they had it to do over an escape from a sticky situation. Senator Lisa Murkowski (R-AK) and other Senate Republicans, after passage of ObamaCare, began discussing how some of ObamaCare was worth saving. Seeking to use ObamaCare as a campaign issue instead of fighting for freedom, Republicans moved on from actually fighting for repeal.

Time and again, Republicans bail on the fight. When Barack Obama used a recess appointment to put champion of redistribution Donald Berwick in charge of Medicare and Medicaid, Republican Senators pounded their chests, claimed they would hold Barack Obama accountable, and then did nothing. When Democrats and John McCain pushed McCain-Feingold, instead of using every parliamentary weapon in the Senate arsenal to kill it, Republicans rolled over, let George W. Bush sign it into law, then prayed the Supreme Court would kill it. The Court by and large declined to do so in the lawsuit that immediately followed passage.[40]

After September 11, 2001, Republicans and Democrats together rushed to create a Department of Homeland Security, which became the third largest department in the Executive Branch.[41] No Republican leader questioned the need to create a complex, burgeoning new bureaucracy through comprehensive legislation pulling together a host of existing and new agencies. When Hurricane Katrina hit Louisiana, and again when British Petroleum's Deep Water Horizon oil platform exploded causing a devasting oil spill, the massive bureaucracy could barely function—but no one has considered serious change.

On October 27, 1964, Ronald Reagan gave one of his most famous speeches, "A Time for Choosing," that even today serves as a guide for the problem Republicans face in their fight, internally and against the Left, to shrink government. In the speech, Reagan said this:

> [T]his idea that government is beholden to the people, that it has no other source of power except the sovereign people, is still the newest and the most unique idea in all the long history of man's relation to man.
>
> This is the issue of this election: Whether we believe in our capacity for self-government or whether we abandon the American revolution and confess that a little intellectual elite in a far-distant capitol can plan our lives for us better than we can plan them ourselves. You and I are told increasingly we have to choose between a left or right. Well I'd like to suggest there is no such thing as a left or right. There's only an up or down—man's [age-old] dream, the ultimate in individual freedom consistent with law and order, or down to the ant heap of totalitarianism...
>
> No government ever voluntarily reduces itself in size. So government programs, once launched, never disappear. Actually, a government bureau is the nearest thing to eternal life we'll ever see on this earth...
>
> You and I have a rendezvous with destiny.
>
> We'll preserve for our children this, the last best hope of man on earth, or we'll sentence them to take the last step into a thousand years of darkness.[42]

Neither government itself nor Republicans will ever shrink the size and scope of government unless conservatives hold their Republican leaders accountable. In doing so, conservatives must learn to discern between people who are actual conservatives and those whose conservative tendencies camouflage their big-government agendas.

CONSERVATIVE?

Lately, we have collectively been saying a lot of people are conservatives, when we should be saying they merely have some conservative beliefs. Here is a good example:

> George W. Bush is not a conservative. He is conservative, but not a conservative. While Christianity has certainly always defined who George Bush is, conservatism has not. Put another way, George W. Bush's gut instinct is a conservative one, but the fiber of his being is not that of a movement conservative.

It was Rush Limbaugh in 2005, notably in a podcast with RedState.com, who was the first real conservative (noun) to say George W. Bush was not a conservative, but had conservative instincts.

Here is where the trouble comes in: there is no rule to separate between the two. On December 10, 2010, Congressman Kevin Brady sent out a press notice that said "House conservatives," not "House Republicans," would hold a press conference on the debt ceiling. The congressmen involved were Steve Scalise (R-LA), Eric Cantor (R-VA), Kevin Brady (R-TX), Jim Jordan (R-OH), John Shimkus (R-IL), Jeb Hensarling (R-TX), Jack Kingston (R-GA), Mike Conaway (R-TX), John Fleming (R-LA), Eric Paulsen (R-MN), Chris Lee (R-NY), and "other House Conservatives."

Each of these men is in some way conservative—meaning they possess some conservative beliefs—but they are not all conservatives. Several on the list are not by definition conservatives, but are by definition Republicans. The Republican party defines them, and conservatism only describes one aspect of their being.

Why bring this up and why bring up an obscure press release from 2009? It's pretty simple really—there are a lot of people out there who call themselves conservatives who are not defined by their conservatism. Many Republicans who have conservative instincts still put their party first. And that is where the relevance is—those more defined by their party put their party first and those more defined by their principles put their principles first. Compare and contrast, say, Jeb Hensarling with John Boehner, or Jim DeMint with Mitch McConnell. Hensarling and DeMint are conservatives first and Republicans second. Boehner and McConnell are Republicans first and conservatives second. Hensarling and DeMint are more likely to fight for the principle and Boehner and McConnell are more likely to fight for an improved position for the party. (Between the two men, Boehner can be said to be more conservative than McConnell as Boehner has never taken an earmark.)

That's not to disparage Boehner and McConnell. It is just reality. Conservatism describes one aspect of them and if they can reconcile a conservative principle with improving their party's position, they will not hesitate to do so.

Conservatives need to do a better job of finding people to run for office who are defined as conservatives, not as party men. It is no secret in Washington that the people who show the most contempt for pro-life activists are not leftists, but Republican establishment leaders who think that, like children, pro-lifers need to be seen and not heard. The establishment thinks life issues do not help advance the GOP. Conservative leaders, however, embrace pro-lifers.

Sure, sure, for those of you who only pay attention to the theater, many a Republican politician pounds the pulpit on abortion, but behind the scenes, when the curtain is down, they do everything they can to block the abortion vote from making it to the floor and into the public square.

Look at the Republican Establishment. Charlie Crist, the Republican turned Independent Governor of Florida is the perfect embodiment of where things stand. One year he is anti-life. The next year he is pro-life. One day he is pro-stimulus. The next day he is anti-stimulus. But it is not just Crist. Across the nation, the Republican Establishment supports people who are not conservatives, but just may have a conservative instinct. Those instincts can change. It is much more difficult to change a total person than to change one attribute of that person. The nation cannot move toward freedom as long as the Republican Party remains controlled by big government statists who try to claim to be "big government conservatives."

No one would believe freedom does not sell in New England. Conservatives fight for freedom. Republicans fight for Republicanism, but few have any idea what that actually means any more.

Unfortunately, there is no hard and fast rule. Two people may arrive at two separate conclusions about whether a politician is a conservative or just has conservative tendencies. It is difficult. But that does not make it impossible. Conservative voters and tea party activists must pay attention to this. The easiest way maybe to think of this that a man defined by his conservatism, like a man defined by his faith, will fight for it. A man who has his faith or his conservatism as just an attribute, has many other attributes he can rely on and will often not fight when he needs to.

If conservatives want to move forward and fight the Democrats (who, unlike the Republican Party, want to profoundly change the American way of life), they must use discernment in choosing candidates. Looking beyond the simple issues for Republicans, like life and tax cuts, to harder issues like earmarks and a willingness to vote no on popular legislation, will help foster discernment as to who the real and viable conservative is. Only then can those who fight for freedom deal with the real menace to our freedom: Barack Obama and the Democrats.

CHAPTER 2

BARACK OBAMA'S WAR AGAINST ALL THINGS SAVE THE REAL ENEMY

The history of totalitarianism is the history of the quest to transcend the human condition and create a society where our deepest meaning and destiny are realized simply by virtue of the fact that we live in it. It cannot be done, and even if, as often is the case of liberal fascism, the effort is very careful to be humane and decent, it will still result in a kind of benign tyranny where some people get to impose their ideas of goodness and happiness on those who may not share them.[1]

—JONAH GOLDBERG, INTRODUCTION TO *LIBERAL FASCISM*

President Obama's chief of staff, Rahm Emanuel, famously declared the Obama Administration would not let a crisis go to waste. In Barack Obama's zeal to remake the United States in his image, he has scored numerous legislative triumphs in his first two years in office. In response, his popularity numbers have plummeted from historic highs, to almost historic lows.

In 2008, Americans voted overwhelmingly for Barack Obama and thought they would forever be able to say we were a nation no longer torn by race. Yet after he was sworn in and began implementing his agenda, the nation started retreating from Barack Obama. Having embraced the ideal of a post-racial America under the mantle of "hope and change," voters were dismayed to discover that socialism was part of the package.

Through domestic legislation, foreign policy, appointments, and presidential statements, Barack Obama is showing more and more that he is not a liberal, but a radical bent on transforming the United States through upheaval of our economy, institutions, traditions, and foreign alliances. As Jonah Goldberg pointed out, this amounts to a fascism the world has seen before, during the militarism of World War II:

> Inspired by ideas like those in William James's famous essay "The Moral Equivalent of War," militarism seemed to provide a workable and sensible model for achieving desirable ends. Mussolini, who openly admired and invoked James, used this logic for his famous "Battle of the Grains" and other sweeping social initiatives. Such ideas had an immense following in the United States, with many leading progressives championing the use of "industrial armies" to create the ideal workers' democracy .... From healthcare to gun control to global warming, liberals insist that we need to "get beyond politics" and "put ideological differences behind us" in order to "do the people's business." The experts and scientists know what to do, we are told; therefore the time for debate is over. This, albeit in a nicer and more benign form, is the logic of fascism.[2]

DOMESTIC POLICY

The Stimulus

Entering office, Barack Obama worked exceedingly hard to get a stimulus bill through Congress. The American Recovery and Reinvestment Act of 2009 sought to distribute $787 billion, but with a catch: the money would be paid out over time, culminating in a giant binge of government disbursements before the 2010 elections, with the remainder to be spent in the early part of 2011.[3]

The money would be allocated with $288 billion for tax benefits, $275 billion for contracts, grants, and loans, and $224 billion for entitlements.[4] In other words, the welfare state would be expanded, and jobs would be created through government spending—a loving embrace of failed Keynesian economics.

During Barack Obama's 2010 State of the Union address,[5] he gave away the game on just how flawed his stimulus was at getting the economy going again. He said, "Because of the steps we took, there are about 2 million Americans working right now who would otherwise be unemployed. 200,000 work in construction and clean energy. 300,000 are teachers and other education workers. Tens of thousands are cops, firefighters, correctional officers, and first responders. And we are on track to add another one and a half million jobs to this total by the end of the year."

Review the list. Every job listed is either a government job or a job so connected to government that it would not exist but for government. The clean energy industry? It owes its very existence to government subsidies. Construction? He is talking about roads and other infrastructure projects, representing government-dependent jobs that will go away once the project is done.

That was just the beginning of his speech. It got much worse.

After these opening salvos, the president said, "I'm proposing that we take $30 billion of the money Wall Street banks have repaid and use it to help community banks give small businesses the credit they need to stay afloat. I am also proposing a new small business tax credit—one that will go to over one million small businesses who hire new workers or raise wages."

First, if the money flowing back to the government is flowing right back out, that remains an expense—leaving the deficit $30 billion worse. Second, why are community banks being targeted? They generally have less capital to lend to small businesses, thereby limiting growth. Why is the government playing favorites with who, in an industry, it assists? Third, why offer a tax credit, i.e. money back off taxes? Why not actually cut the tax rate on small businesses? Why not end the corporate income tax, which is now higher than almost every single one of our international competitors? After all, the president did say, "If America sits on the sidelines while other nations sign trade deals, we will lose the chance to create jobs on our shores."[6] Many countries are competing with the United States through sharply reduced corporate income taxes.

The president also said, "we can put Americans to work today building the infrastructure of tomorrow. From the first railroads to the interstate highway system, our nation has always been built to compete. There's no reason Europe or China should have the fastest trains, or the new factories that manufacture clean energy products" and "You see, Washington has been telling us to wait for decades, even as the problems have grown worse. Meanwhile, China's not waiting to revamp its economy. Germany's not waiting. India's not waiting."

This again assumes a dependence on government jobs and infrastructure. The comparison to China is, in fact, frightening. China is a command and control economy. What the communist leaders want, the communist leaders get. China was able to build its high speed train system in record time by ignoring every law on the books pertaining to worker safety, environmental hazards, and more.

More troubling though, a few days after the State of the Union address, Barack Obama released his budget and admitted that "by design" unemployment remained high:

"All told, as of the end of November 2009, about 50 percent of Recovery Act funds—or $395 billion—has been either obligated or is providing assistance directly to Americans in the form of tax relief. By design, the bulk of the remaining 50 percent of Recovery Act funds will be deployed in the coming months of 2010 and during the beginning of 2011 to support additional job creation when our economy continues to need a boost."[7]

If the point of the stimulus plan was to create jobs, it seems curious that the government would spend the funds to create jobs so slowly. After all, during his State of the Union address, Barack Obama said, "Experts from across the political spectrum warned that if we did not act, we might face a second depression. So we acted—immediately and aggressively. And one year later, the worst of the storm has passed."

"The worst of the storm has passed"? Really? On February 5, 2010, more than a week after Barack Obama's State of the Union address, Peter Goodman reported in the *New York Times*, "The unemployment rate unexpectedly dipped to 9.7 percent in January, from 10 percent in December, the government reported Friday, buoying hopes that the worst job market in at least a quarter-century is finally improving."[8] Note the use of the word "unexpectedly."

What Obama's State of the Union completely ignored was the fact that when measured by his own projections, his so-called stimulus was a flop. On January 9, 2009, while he was still trying to get his plan through Congress, his nominee to head up the Council of Economic Advisers released a report that included a chart depicting the "Unemployment Rate With and Without the Recovery Plan." Unemployment was supposed to peak at 8 percent in the third quarter of 2009 if the Recovery package was passed. If nothing was done (which they considered a bad thing), unemployment was estimated to peak at around 9.1 percent in early 2010.[9]

Unemployment hit 10.1 percent in October 2010—an entire point above what his team said it was supposed to be if we had done nothing—and remains higher than the worst-case scenario Obama's team could come up with if their plan wasn't implemeted.[10] Imagine how bad it would have been if Obama had been trying to make it worse.

ObamaCare

Much is written in this book about ObamaCare, but there are a few points to consider.

First, ObamaCare was passed despite the loud protestations of the American public. Barack Obama brought back Bill Clinton to sell the Senate Democrats on healthcare. Bill Clinton made the case that if the Democrats passed ObamaCare, unlike 1994, they would not be swept from office. Likewise, speaking to Andrea Mitchell on MSNBC, Iowa Democratic Senator Tom Harkin said, "If the Republicans...thought this was going to be devastating to the Democrats, they'd be sitting back rubbing their hands saying 'go ahead and do it.'"[11] The Democrats may have bought it, but it was to their detriment politically.

Second, the Democrats made one of the hallmarks of their legislation the "individual mandate." The whole of ObamaCare rests on an individual mandate—forcing American citizens to buy health insurance. "When Congress required most Americans to obtain health insurance[12] or pay a penalty, Democrats denied that they were creating a new tax. But in court, the Obama administration and its allies now defend the requirement as an exercise of the government's 'power to lay and collect taxes.'"[13]

Lastly, American businesses are only now beginning to understand just how devastating ObamaCare will be to them. One of the program's provisions assesses a penalty on companies whose employees expend more than 9.5 percent of their household income on company-provided healthcare insurance. As the *Weekly Standard* noted, "White Castle, which currently provides insurance to all of its full-time workers and picks up 70 to 89 percent of their premium costs, believes it will likely end up paying those penalties. The financial hit will make it hard for the company to maintain its 421 restaurants, let alone create new jobs, says company spokesman Jamie Richardson." The company expects this penalty to consume 55 percent of its net income.[14]

The IRS itself, months after ObamaCare passed, noted just how burdensome it will be to small businesses. As CNN reported, "The new regulations, which kick in at the start of 2012, require any taxpayer with business income to issue 1099 forms to all vendors from whom they purchased more than $600 of goods and services that year. That promises to launch a fusillade of new paperwork: An estimated 40 million taxpayers will be subject to the requirement, including 26 million who run sole proprietorships, according to a report released this week by National Taxpayer Advocate Nina Olson."[15]

The Taxpayer Advocate Service's Fiscal Year 2011 Objectives Report to Congress contained this alarming passage:

A provision in the Patient Protection and Affordable Care Act (PPACA),[16] enacted in March of this year, added a new information reporting requirement that may present significant administrative challenges to taxpayers and the IRS. In particular, businesses will have to issue Forms 1099 for goods purchased after 2011, regardless of the corporate form of the vendor. The Office of the Taxpayer Advocate is concerned that the new reporting burden, particularly as it falls on small businesses, may turn out to be disproportionate as compared with any resulting improvement in tax compliance....

The PPACA provision would apply to businesses of all sizes, charities and other tax-exempt organizations, and government entities. These would include, as reflected in IRS data, 26 million non-farm sole proprietorships, four million S corporations, two million C corporations, three million partnerships, two million farming businesses, one million charities and other tax-exempt organizations, and probably more than 100,000 federal, state, and local government entities. This mass of persons making payments in the course of a trade or business will soon be required to issue information reports to sellers of goods as well as providers of services. They also will have to report payments to a for-profit corporate service provider. In addition, a business will soon be required to report payments for purchases of goods as well as property of any sort. This new requirement has generated a great deal of concern because of its potential to create administrative burdens for businesses, vendors, and the IRS.[17]

Those "administrative burdens" will either become so burdensome that businesses fail, or they will be passed on to consumers in the form of higher prices for goods and services.

Republicans had predicted the measure would be economically devastating. Bill Clinton announced that healthcare was "an economic imperative" while urging Democratic Senators to vote for ObamaCare.[18] We're already discovering who was right.

Welfare Expansion

One of Obama's first acts as president was to undermine welfare reform through the "stimulus" bill with a back-door provision rewarding states that increase their welfare caseloads. Then his FY2011 budget, released in 2010, contained proposals that would completely undermine the 1996 welfare reform bill—which had been massively successful at cutting costs and helping recipients. In fact, welfare reform may be the only federal program that cost less in 2010 (in inflation-adjusted dollars—$17.9 billion) than in 2000—$19.8 billion.[19]

As reported by the Heritage Foundation, "President Obama's budget seeks to...create a new funding system to reward states for increasing the size of their welfare caseloads," which would return the federal government "to the failed pre-reform policy of rewarding states for increasing welfare dependence."

The budget also seeks to "eliminate the only remaining federal program to strengthen marriage at a time when the unwed birth rate is approaching 40 percent," by eliminating "all funding for the Marriage and Fatherhood grant program, which has served to advance and encourage healthy marriages in low-income communities and strengthen relationships between fathers and children. Despite the fact that the collapse of marriage is the prime cause of child poverty and welfare dependence, the Obama Administration plans to terminate all federal activity designed to strengthen marriage. Instead, Obama will dramatically expand the over $300 billion the government spends each year subsidizing single parenthood. His Administration will also continue government welfare policies that penalize lower income couples that do marry."[20]

Obama has also penalized marriage in the ObamaCare bill: many couples will have lower healthcare costs by not marrying and just remaining single.

Diana Furchtgott-Roth of the Hudson Institute remarked that the subsidies are structured so that two people can get more government money as singles rather than as a married couple. Using an example of two people making $43,000 each, she illustrates that as singles, they both qualify for subsidies, but if they marry, their combined earnings of $86,000 far exceed the $58,000 cut-off for aid to a couple. For older couples, the effect is more pronounced: two individuals in their sixties making a combined $60,000 would receive an additional $10,425 to purchase insurance if they become or remain single.[21]

Who suffers most from marriage penalties? Single mothers. They make up 45 percent of all families living in poverty. For the sake of these women and their children, Washington should be embracing policies that encourage marriage, rather than punish it.[22] These are the most recent ways Washington has decided to use your tax dollars against you. Obama likes to portray himself as a great family man. But his policies are anything but family friendly.

Financial Reform Legislation

In a private meeting at the White House in April, Barack Obama summoned the CEOs of America's most powerful financial institutions and told them, "My administration is the only thing between you and the pitchforks."[23] One of the attendees commented to *Politico*, "The signal from Obama's body language and demeanor was, 'I'm the president, and you're not.'"

Concurrent to Barack Obama's "good cop" routine with the CEO's, the AFL-CIO announced it was marching on Wall Street, no doubt driving home the pitchforks message.

Conventional wisdom suggests that the current recession is a by-product of government's failure to effectively regulate financial markets and institutions. The horrendous new federal financial regulatory monster, misnamed "Restoring American Financial Stability Act of 2010," spearheaded by Senator Chris Dodd (D-CT) and Representative Barney Frank (D-MA), did nothing to discipline the major miscreants in this tragedy: "Freddie Mac" (Federal Home Loan Mortgage Corporation) and "Fannie Mae" (Federal National Mortgage Association). Certainly, many private investment firms—led by Goldman Sachs—share heavily in the blame, but our own federal government was at ground zero in precipitating this debacle.

How did Washington create the financial train-wreck? By encouraging Freddie and Fannie, two government-sponsored enterprises (GSEs) to hand out mortgage loans to demonstrably unqualified borrowers in the name of social justice. While these organizations are ostensibly private companies, having sold ownership in themselves to private stockholders since 1968, their status as GSEs conveyed the implication that when in trouble, Fannie and Freddie would be bailed out by the United States Treasury (i.e., all of us as taxpayers.) In his book *Financial Fiasco*, Johan Norberg confirms our worst fears about these mortgage monsters: "A GSE is potentially the most dangerous type of enterprise since it may allow private owners to take any risks they can imagine, pocket any profits for themselves, but count on tax-payers to take care of any losses."[24]

These GSEs hold trillions of dollars worth of mortgages. "Together [Freddie and Fannie] own or guarantee almost 31 million home loans worth about $5.5 trillion. That's about half of all mortgages," reports Associated Press financial analyst Alan Ziebel.[25] When the mortgage activities of the Federal Housing Administration (FHA) and the Veterans Administration are included, nearly 100 percent of home loans in the first quarter of 2010 were made or guaranteed by United States taxpayers.[26] And, Freddie/Fannie use their political clout and extensive lobbying on Capitol Hill to continuously expand their reach. Over the years, many political heavyweights have cycled through the management ranks of Freddie and Fannie, including Obama's Chief of Staff Rahm Emanuel, and have been well rewarded financially and politically.

It could have been averted. In 2005, Senate Republicans became concerned about the lending practices of Freddie/Fannie. They sought to impose tough lending standards and liquidity and capital requirements on Freddie/Fannie to reduce their financial risk. All Democrats, including then Senator Barack Obama, opposed and defeated the measure, which required sixty votes. (As a senator, Obama was the third-largest recipient of campaign contributions from Freddie/Fannie).[27] The Freddie/Fannie disaster that confronts American tax-payers—a bailout that may reach a trillion dollars—could have been averted.

Despite President Obama's tough talk about special interests, the financial industry, and its powerful lobby having opposed safeguards against reckless risks and bad practices that led to the financial crisis, Obama and Senate Democrats have refused to include any financial control on Freddie/Fannie in the new financial regulatory bill.

It is high time the United States government got completely out of the home (and other) mortgage business. Treasury's de facto "ownership"/operation of Freddie and Fannie since September 2008 gives Congress the power to spin off Freddie and Fannie to the private sector, ending all subsidies and guarantees. To do so would require deep discounting of the GSEs' loan portfolios, but better to rid ourselves of this burden now than allow the liberals to keep playing "social justice" politics at taxpayer expense.

CRONY CAPITALISM

Freddie and Fannie didn't act alone in creating the mortgage meltdown that has thrown the world into recession and undermined home values and the net worth of millions of Americans. It took cronies on Wall Street to purchase the sub-prime loans, bundle them into huge packages of securitized debt (collateralized debt obligations), and market them worldwide to largely unsuspecting purchasers. Why would we say "unsuspecting"? Because these packages of what turned out to be "toxic" mortgages were given top approvals by Standard & Poors, Moody's, and other United States-government-approved "rating agencies."

The only problem is nobody really monitored the rating agencies, and they were incentivized to give favorable ratings to the financial "products" of the investment houses which paid their fees. There is no question but that the rating agencies bear a tremendous responsibility for the sub-prime-mortgage-precipitated recession.

Then there was the role played by Treasury Secretary Henry Paulson, who started the whole "too big to fail" domino effect. As past Chairman of Goldman Sachs, he had millions of dollars of Goldman shares in a blind trust. If Goldman had been allowed to fail, his retirement assets and income would have been impacted. He let Bear Stearns and Lehman go into bankruptcy, but Goldman survived.

Goldman was threatened because Goldman managers took their pound of flesh in 2007. For example, Paulson's successor, Floyd Blankfein, walked in 2007 with a compensation package of $68 million when he had to know he sat atop a house of cards. How could he have had such a deal? Because the compensation schedule gave bonuses to traders like Blankfein even when the end was near.

Meanwhile, Goldman, knowing it was selling packages of mortgage-backed securities that were very likely to fail, began "selling short," i.e., betting against the very mortgage securities it was selling to its customers worldwide. This may be one of the most egregious violations of fiduciary responsibilities ever observed in a not overly ethical Wall Street environment. This may set a new standard for "screw thy neighbor." And yet the new financial regulatory bill does nothing to staunch this practice precisely because Goldman and other Wall Street firms have been lining the political pockets of Obama and the liberals who do their bidding in the Senate. These are the people who must be exposed for their duplicity and millions in campaign contributions to Obama, Harry Reid, and company.

In the future, we must short-circuit a replay of the last Goldman-Sachs rescue effort. Treasury was considering letting AIG go into bankruptcy. But Goldman Sachs' representatives at the table let it be known that AIG owed them about $13 billion and that Goldman's survival might hang in the balance. In light of that, about $62 billion of new bailout money was made available to AIG, which paid multiple foreign banks—as well as Goldman—100 cents on the dollar, rather than negotiating a "hair cut" for all.

Recent testimony by Joseph Cassano, who ran AIG's shop known as AIGFP that handled credit default swaps on the mortgage-backed securities it insured, has put the taxpayer rescue of Goldman-Sachs in proper perspective. Cassano, who left AIG in March 2008, commented on the Fall '08 bailout of AIG in which Goldman and a number of foreign banks were paid 100 cents on the dollar. As reported by the *Wall Street Journal*,

> As part of the bailout, banks were compensated in full on
> $62 billion in swaps in a move that helped stop AIG's cash

bleed but caused the company to realize large losses. Mr. Cassano said things might have turned out differently, had he not been asked to leave AIG. When Goldman Sachs demanded collateral from AIGFP while he was running the division, he said, his team asserted its rights under the swaps contracts and challenged the lower prices for the bonds being provided by the Wall Street firm. Following negotiations with Goldman, AIG often posted less collateral than the bank had initially requested, he said. If he was still at AIGFP in the fall of 2008, he said, he would have taken a similarly tough line with banks' mounting collateral demands and prevented taxpayers from having to compensate the firm's counterparties in full. "I would have been able to negotiate a substantial discount by using the rights available to us such that the taxpayer would not have had to accelerate the $40 billion to the counterparties," Mr. Cassano said Wednesday, referring to some of the money paid to banks to close out the swaps contracts.[28]

Goldman apparently had to have 100 cents on the dollar at that time to survive. Bankruptcy was good enough for Bear Stearns and Lehman Brothers, but their clout at Treasury wasn't quite the same as Goldman's.

But somehow, that wasn't the lesson learned when it came time for a financial "reform" package. In his never-ending quest to overthrow the U.S. economy and free market, Barack Obama agitated for a financial reform package that is filled with the kinds of delightful left-wing nonsense most people would assume are jokes, except they really are in the legislation.

Title III of the legislation requires that "each [federal] agency shall establish an Office of Minority and Women Inclusion that shall be responsible for all matters of the agency relating to diversity in management, employment, and business activities."[29] What that has to do with financial reform is anyone's guess.

Title V of the legislation expanded access to insurance for minorities in under-served areas, much like the Community Reinvestment Act did for housing, which precipitated the housing crisis.

The legislation set aside Fannie Mae and Freddie Mac for special treatment, yet again. It also expanded regulations on the oil and natural gas industries.

Most troubling, despite tea party activists around the nation waking up upon passage of TARP and the bank bailouts, the financial reform legislation created a permanent bailout authority and allowed the federal government to delve further into the regulation of free markets, which are decidedly less free after passage of the legislation.

As negotiations were winding down on the legislation, Senator Chris Dodd told reporters, "No one will know until this is actually in place how it works. But we believe we've done something that has been needed for a long time. It took a crisis to bring us to the point where we could *actually get this job done*"[30] (emphasis added). Just like ObamaCare.

The Net Result of Obama's Domestic Hope and Change

A March 1, 2010, article by Patrice Hill in the *Washington Times* noted that more Americans had become dependent on government than at any other time in American history.[31] "[F]or the first time since the Great Depression, Americans took more aid from the government than they paid in taxes," Ms. Hill wrote.

Likewise, the Heritage Foundation's 2010 Index of Dependence on Government found a dramatic rise in dependence on government. The foundation noted, "Americans' dependence on the government was 14 times greater in 2009 than it was in 1962."[32]

The Brookings Institute issued a report in July 2010 with a dreary picture of the future. "If future job growth continues at a rate of roughly 208,000 jobs per month, the average monthly job creation for the best year for job creation in the 2000s, [recovery] would take 136 months (more than 11 years). In a more optimistic scenario, with 321,000 jobs created per month, the average monthly job creation for the best year in the 1990s, it would take over 57 months (almost 5 years)."[33]

According to Barack Obama, that's good news.

FOREIGN AFFAIRS

At home, Barack Obama has overseen an expanding federal government taking over, with ObamaCare alone, one-sixth of the American economy. Coming into office promising to make America respected again abroad after eight years of George W. Bush, it is more and more clear Barack Obama has done his best to realign the United States with its enemies.

The only explanation of his conduct in foreign affairs is to understand that Barack Obama believes the United States is too big and too powerful, and we should just be one of 196 countries.

The Honduras & Iranian Affairs

The Honduran people, wise to the ways of Latin American politics, adopted a constitution that prohibits any president from serving more than one term. Presidents in Latin American countries, like herpes and Jimmy Carter, have a habit of never going away. Further, the Honduran constitution requires that any referenda put to the voters be approved by the Honduran Congress.

The Hondurans are so concerned about potential despots, Article 239 of their constitution states that any president who proposes extending his term in office is automatically removed from office. Article 313 of the Honduran constitution allows their Supreme Court to deputize the Honduran military to carry out its orders, including removing politicians from office who seek to extend a president's term.

Ignoring the constitution, in mid-2009, President Manuel Zelaya, a man less popular in Honduras than George W. Bush was when he left office in this country, ordered a "non-binding" referendum be put to the voters on extending his stay in office.

Glenn Garvin wrote in the *Miami Herald*, "After the Honduran supreme court ruled that only the country's congress could call such an election, Zelaya ordered the army to help him stage it anyway.... When the head of the armed forces, acting on orders from the supreme court, refused, Zelaya fired him, then led a mob to break into a military base where the ballots were stored."

The Honduran Supreme Court, Congress, Attorney General, and members of Zelaya's cabinet opposed his move as unconstitutional. The Supreme Court ordered the military to remove Zelaya from office on June 28, 2009. Honduras has no impeachment process as we know it.

Last December, the Honduran vice president resigned. No replacement had been named. The Honduran constitution requires that in such circumstances, the head of Congress become provisional president, much like our Speaker of the House would become president if both Joe Biden and Barack Obama were unavailable.

Roberto Micheletti, a member of Zelaya's own political party, became president of Honduras. Despite protests from Zelaya's supporters, the nation's trade unions, business groups, the Catholic Church, and most citizens supported Zelaya's ouster—no one wanted a tyrant, let alone one propped up by drug lords and marxist thugs like Hugo Chavez and Fidel Castro.

Nonetheless, Barack Obama declared the Honduran government's actions a coup—never mind the government was preserving its democracy instead of overthrowing it. Secretary of State Hillary Clinton said, "The action taken against Honduran President Mel Zelaya violates the precepts of the Inter-American Democratic Charter, and thus should be condemned by all."[34] She called on Hondurans to uphold their constitutional processes, the very thing they were doing by ousting Zelaya.

On June 4, 2009, Barack Obama said from Egypt, "No system of government can or should be imposed on one nation by any other."[35] Shortly thereafter, Iran held elections that caused widespread popular protests. Members of Congress expressed solidarity with the protestors.

On June 16, 2009, after critics said Barack Obama was doing nothing to address the Iranian crisis, Obama said in the White House Rose Garden, "How that plays out over the next several days and several weeks is something ultimately for the Iranian people to decide." He went on to say, "It's not productive given the history of U.S.-Iranian relations to be seen as meddling."[36] As with his campaign promises, our president quickly forgot his own words.

Barack Obama more quickly condemned President Zelaya's ouster by a democratic government than he condemned Iran for gunning down its citizens who had taken to the streets to demand freedom. Obama needed public pressure to even discuss Iran.

The "Special Relationship"

At Westminster College in Fulton, Missouri, on March 5, 1946, Sir Winston Churchill gave a speech he called "The Sinews of Peace." The speech coined two terms of importance to the late twentieth and early twenty-first centuries. First, he described what he called an "iron curtain" being lowered across Eastern Europe. Second, he described the British and American relationship as a "special relationship," saying,

> Neither the sure prevention of war, nor the continuous rise of world organization will be gained without what I have called the fraternal association of the English-speaking peoples. This means a special relationship between the British Commonwealth and Empire and the United States. This is no time for generalities, and I will venture to be precise. Fraternal association requires not only the growing friendship and mutual

understanding between our two vast but kindred systems of society, but the continuance of the intimate relationship between our military advisers, leading to common study of potential dangers, the similarity of weapons and manuals of instructions, and to the interchange of officers and cadets at technical colleges.[37]

Since that speech, the "special relationship" has been often referred to, but Barack Obama's routine engagements with the United Kingdom of Great Britain and Northern Ireland suggest he doesn't buy into the notion of a special relationship. In fact, shortly after entering office, Barack Obama returned to Britain a famous Jacob Epstein bronze bust of Winston Churchill. Former British Prime Minister Tony Blair gave the bust to George W. Bush "as a loan" after September 11, 2001, and it remained in the Oval Office through Bush's presidency. Gordon Brown, the British Prime Minister serving upon Obama's entry to the presidency, offered to let the bust stay in the Oval Office, but Barack Obama declined.[38]

The British took the return as a snub. Tom Baldwin, writing for the *Times* of London, noted, "Mr Obama shows little evidence of the Anglophilia that led his predecessors to pepper speeches with quotations from Churchill. Instead, there have been suggestions that he has reason to disdain the former Prime Minister. In 1952 Churchill declared the Kenya emergency in the homeland of Mr Obama's father, sending in troops to crush the Mau Mau rebellion against colonial rule. Among the Kenyans who were detained without trial and allegedly tortured by the British was Hussein Onyango Obama, the President's grandfather."[39]

When visiting Queen Elizabeth II at Buckingham Palace in 2009, Barack Obama famously gave her an iPod, but made sure not to bow before the monarch, as no American president should. Subsequently, Barack Obama bowed to the king of Saudi Arabia, the emperor of

Japan, and the Chinese Premier.[40] The White House denied the bow to the king of Saudi Arabia.[41]

In March 2009, Barack Obama entertained Gordon Brown at the White House for the first time and declined to have a formal press conference, which the Brits again took as a snub. During the visit, Prime Minister Brown gave President Obama several gifts, including a wooden pen holder made from a warship that had been used to eradicate the slave trade. In return, President Obama gifted the Prime Minister with a collection of DVDs that the British press reported could not be played on British DVD players.[42]

British officials told the *Telegraph*, "Obama aides seemed unfamiliar with the expectations that surround a major visit by a British prime minister."[43] The paper also reported, "A well-connected Washington figure, who is close to members of Mr. Obama's inner circle, expressed concern that Mr. Obama had failed so far to 'even fake an interest in foreign policy.'"[44] A State Department official, when asked about the event, told the *Telegraph*, "There's nothing special about Britain. You're just the same as the other 190 countries in the world. You shouldn't expect special treatment."[45] It's disheartening that Obama's State department doesn't seem to know that the United States recognizes 194 countries—as their own website acknowledges.[46] (Perhaps these facts remain posted from the previous administration?)

In September 2009, at the G-20 Summit in Pittsburgh, PA, Barack Obama and Gordon Brown had another embarrassing encounter. Patrick Wintour, in the *Guardian* on September 24, 2009, wrote, "Gordon Brown lurched from being hailed as a global statesman to intense embarrassment tonight, after it emerged U.S. President Barack Obama had turned down no fewer than five requests from Downing Street to hold a bilateral meeting at the United Nations in New York or at the G20 summit starting in Pittsburgh today."[47]

If that weren't bad enough, in February 2010, the Obama Administration refused to back Great Britain in a territorial dispute with

Argentina over the Falkland Islands—a group of islands Margaret Thatcher's government defended in a war with Argentina in 1982.

Great Britain placed an oil platform 100 miles from the Falkland Islands coastline, and the Argentine President began working to obstruct supplies to the oil platform. Thirty-two Latin American nations signed on to a statement agreeing to support "the legitimate rights of the republic of Argentina in the sovereignty dispute with Great Britain." Hugo Chavez, Venezuela's dictator, declared, "If conflict breaks out, be sure Argentina will not be alone like it was back then."[48]

The Obama Administration decided to stay neutral in the matter. A State Department spokesman said, "We are aware not only of the current situation but also of the history, but our position remains one of neutrality. The US recognizes *de facto* UK administration of the islands but takes no position on the sovereignty claims of either party."[49]

Trashing the Dalai Lama

In February 2010, the Dalai Lama called on the White House. Since his flight from the Communists in 1959, the Dalai Lama has continued to serve as the head of the Tibetan government-in-exile and is viewed as a spiritual leader by millions around the world. However, China does not like the Dalai Lama.

What do you do when you are Barack Obama (who famously bowed to the Chinese Premier), and the Dalai Lama comes calling at the White House? After the meeting, the White House ushered the Dalai Lama out through the trash door. Brian Williams, on *NBC Nightly News* for February 19, 2010, described the event like this:

> How do you ask the Dalai Lama to leave the White House if you're trying to keep his visit from becoming too public? Well, judging from the trash bags that he had to walk around, the Obama White House had him exit through a door seldom

used by anybody but household staff. It's where the West Wing meets the main residence. China, however, did notice the visit and called in the U.S. ambassador to China today to protest.[50]

Israel and Obama

Jewish voters are a key demographic for Democrats, and they are not thrilled by Barack Obama's treatment of Israel. Although at a July 2010 press conference at the White House, both Barack Obama and Israeli Prime Minister Benjamin Netanyahu proclaimed the U.S.–Israel relationship as strong as ever, press reports suggest otherwise.

At a March 2010 meeting between the Israeli Prime Minister and the White House, things did not go so well. Vice President Joe Biden intentionally showed up ninety minutes late to a dinner with the Israeli Prime Minister.[51] Two weeks later at his meeting with the Israeli Prime Minister, President Obama "immediately presented Mr. Netanyahu with a list of 13 demands designed both to end the feud with his administration and to build Palestinian confidence ahead of the resumption of peace talks.... When the Israeli prime minister stalled, Mr. Obama rose from his seat declaring: 'I'm going to the residential wing to have dinner with Michelle and the girls.'"[52]

The Net Result of Obama's Foreign Policy Blunders

Barack Obama, upon securing the votes to become the Democratic Presidential Nominee in 2008, gave a speech in St. Paul, Minnesota, saying, "We will be able to look back and tell our children that this was the moment when we began to provide care for the sick and good jobs to the jobless; this was the moment when the rise of the oceans began to slow and our planet began to heal; this was the moment when we ended a war and secured our nation and restored our image as the last, best hope on earth."[53] We have instead become an international joke.

Our old allies wonder if we still have their back. Our enemies are still our enemies, but they are perfectly happy to have Barack Obama photo-ops to use for propaganda back home. We are more in debt to China than ever before. The world is a far more dangerous place.

NATIONAL SECURITY

In the classic movie *Jurassic Park*, the scientists discover that among the varied dinosaurs at the park are Velociraptors. Dr. Grant, who has studied the creatures, and his partner Ellie ask Robert Multon, the game warden, about their habits. From the script:

> MULDOON: They show extreme intelligence, even problem solving. Especially the big one. We bred eight originally, but when she came in, she took over the pride and killed all but two of the others. That one—when she looks at you, you can see she's thinking (or) working things out. She's the reason we have to feed 'em like this. She had them all attacking the fences when the feeders came.
>
> ELLIE: The fences are electrified, right?
>
> MULDOON: That's right. But they never attack the same place twice. They were testing the fences for weaknesses. Systematically. They remembered.

In Little Rock, Arkansas, a Muslim under investigation after returning from Yemen gunned down army recruiters.[54]

On July 25, 2009, in Denver, CO, an Afghan-American went into a beauty supply store to begin building a bomb to blow up New York. Again.[55]

In Ft. Hood, Texas, a soldier gunned down his fellow soldiers after having had a stint in Yemen.[56]

In New York City, an empty van sat with forged law enforcement documents for two days before New Years Day 2010. We know very little else about that incident.[57]

In the air over Detriot, MI, a Nigerian trained in Yemen tried to blow up a plane. He appears to have been helped to board in Amsterdam without a passport. The passengers on the plane saw another man arrested when they landed in Detroit, but the authorities denied it, then said it was someone from a different flight. Passengers disputed this.[58]

Then we had the attack on the CIA in Afghanistan by a soldier ranked highly enough to get to them without pre-screening. Yemen warns of hundreds more. This all happened in a period of six months from mid-2009 to January 2010.[59]

On Saturday, May 1, 2010, Faisal Shahzad parked a 1993 Nissan Pathfinder in Times Square. Shahzad had constructed a car bomb with propane, gasoline, and fireworks. Luckily, it failed to go off.[60]

Under George W. Bush, leading scholars and pundits declared al Qaeda marginalized. By 2003, the pontiffs of miasmatic beltway wisdom were nearly unanimous that al Qaeda was near dismantled.[61] Like the Velociraptors in *Jurrasic Park*, it seems our enemies are not only not extinct, but are testing the fences for weaknesses. With Barack Obama, they keep finding those weaknesses.

Making America Less Safe

On Christmas Day, 2009, Northwest Airlines (now Delta) Flight 253 carried 278 passengers from Amsterdam to Detroit. As the plane flew through American airspace, Umar Farouk Abdul Mutallab, attempted to blow himself up with a bomb in his underwear. He was not successful.

Mutallab made it onto the airplane and ignited his bomb despite the United States having known for at least two years that he might have terrorist ties.[62] Within twenty-four hours of his attempted bombing, a "Senior Administration Official" at the White House was pointing out that the terrorist watch list had been created by the Bush Administration. After his detention, the United States Government read Mutallab his Miranda Rights instead of treating him like an enemy combatant.

Despite howls of protest, the Obama Administration stood by its decision to treat Mutallab as a common criminal.

Betraying the Military and Intelligence Communities

Upon coming into office, Barack Obama refused to retain General Michael Hayden, a career military man appointed to head the CIA by George W. Bush. Obama instead nominated John O. Brennan, but upon outraged cries from the Left, dropped him in favor of Leon Panetta. Additionally, the Justice Department began investigating whether to prosecute Bush Administration officials and intelligence operatives who had participated in enhanced interrogation of enemy combatants and terrorists.

Within the military, Barack Obama appointed left-wing social change agents more likely to want to advocate gender equality and affirmative action than do what's best for national security. Going against the advice of chiefs of the branches within the military, Barack Obama decided to rescind "Don't Ask, Don't Tell." Prior to that, Barack Obama decided to change course in Afghanistan, but delayed meeting his hand-picked general, General McChrystal. Then, after McChrystal gave an unflattering interview to *Rolling Stone* magazine, Obama fired him only to replace him with General Petraeus whom Democrats, including Joe Biden, had roundly attacked during the Bush Administration.

The low-level guys in both intelligence and defense, the Jack Bauers if you will, are seeing all of this. They saw George W. Bush who made tough decisions in secret and stood by those decisions when they became public, even though those decisions were hugely unpopular.

The low-level guys intrinsically knew they could kill bad men in undisclosed locations and be supported if the lights came on.

These same men see Barack Obama unwilling to stand behind one of their own—a career CIA officer in John O. Brennan—when the Left howls, and they see Barack Obama willing to investigate their own for possible prosecution. It is an unspoken message to all of them that, should they take the bold action needed to keep freedom secure, they may not be backed up by President Obama.

They will therefore return to their state of being prior to September 11. And darkness will again start creeping from the shadows.

Barack Obama is playing a dangerous game—a game that will probably see many of us killed. And we should not be shy about saying so.

APPOINTMENTS: WAR THROUGH COURT AND REGULATION

Barack Obama, being a true radical, intends to bring radical change not just through legislation, but through the courts and regulatory process as well. In so doing, he has nominated leftists for major positions, some of whom are more radical than himself. Here's a sampling.

Donald Berwick

Over objections of Senate Republicans, Barack Obama used a recess appointment to put Donald Berwick in charge of the Centers for Medicare and Medicaid Services, which is essentially the largest insurance company in the United States, covering all Medicare and Medicaid patients. Mr. Berwick is pretty openly a socialist.

On the use of healthcare to redistribute wealth, Mr. Berwick said, "Any healthcare funding plan that is just, equitable, civilized, and humane must, must redistribute wealth from the richer among us to the poorer and the less fortunate. Excellent healthcare is by definition redistribution."[63] Berwick also condemned the American healthcare system because of its dependence on consumer choice.

Robert Chatigny

Barack Obama nominated Judge Robert N. Chatigny to the Second Circuit Court of Appeals. Much of the controversy around Judge Chatigny comes from his presiding over the case of murderer Michael Ross. In questioning Chatigny before the Senate Judiciary Committee, Senator Tom Coburn (R-OK) summed up the objections.

> While in prison, Michael Ross participated in the creation of a documentary on serial killers entitled "The Serial Killers" during which he described in great detail how he raped and murdered eight women and girls. In the video Ross explains: "Serial killers like to strangle their victims and that is, I guess, the most common form of killing because there is more of a connection, it's more real, and it's not as quick."
>
> He later describes how he tied up Leslie Shelley (age 14) and put her in the trunk of his car and then: "took the other girl, April Bernaise (age 14), out and I raped her and killed her and I put her in the front seat."
>
> Then, he pulled Leslie Shelley out of the trunk and brutally killed her.
>
> In describing his last victim, Wendy Baribeault (17), he said: "I raped her and I killed her. It wasn't pleasant; it wasn't a nice rape."
>
> Judge Chatigny, this is the man who you described as "the least culpable of the people on death row" and said the [sic] "he never should have been convicted. Or if convicted, he never should have been sentenced to death" and that "when [Ross] says, I feel that I'm the victim of a miscarriage of justice,

because they didn't treat [Ross's sexual sadism] as a mitigating factor, I can well understand where he's coming from."[64]

Kevin Jennings

Kevin Jennings is Barack Obama's "Safe Schools Czar." He wrote the foreword to a book called *Queering Elementary Education*. The book advocates aggressive homosexual agenda among elementary school students. From the book: "Queering education happens when we look at schooling upside down and view childhood from the inside out."[65] No irony is intended apparently in that description.

Jennings is also a strong opponent of the Boy Scouts of America and, according to the *Washington Times*, encouraged a homosexual relationship between a 15-year-old boy and a much older man who, the boy reported to Jennings, picked the boy up in a bus station bathroom and promptly took the boy home.[66]

Van Jones

Perhaps the most famous of Barack Obama's czars, thanks to Glenn Beck, Van Jones was President Obama's "Green Jobs Czar" until his resignation.

"Jones himself stated in a 2005 interview his environmental activism was a means to fight for racial and class 'justice,' and that he was a 'rowdy black nationalist,' and a 'communist.'"[67]

To put Van Jones in greater perspective, consider just these three points:

He is a 9/11 truther. Jones "signed a statement for 911Truth.org in 2004 demanding an investigation into what the Bush Administration may have done that 'deliberately allowed 9/11 to happen, perhaps as a pretext for war.'"[68]

He believes that "white polluters" steered poison into black neighborhoods.[69]

He also, in 2009 prior to his appointment, attended a forum to promote Barack Obama's agenda and, when asked how Republicans were able to block Obama's agenda, repeatedly called them a–holes. He then said people around Barack Obama would need to get "uppity" to deal with the Republicans.[70]

Cass Sunstein

Writing on January 15, 2010, Glenn Greenwald at *Salon* noted Barack Obama's new head of the Office of Information and Regulatory Affairs, Cass Sunstein, had championed creating fake websites and using outside 501(c)(3) interest groups to act as alleged independent champions of government policy and to "cognitively infiltrate" opposition webstes, etc.[71]

In other words, Cass Sunstein has favored the government using outside parties as government propaganda agents to paint their opposition as fringe and undermine their credibility. Kind of like what has been happening with the tea party movement—lots of union members pretending to be tea party activists causing violence in front of TV cameras. "Sunstein advocates that the Government's stealth infiltration should be accomplished by sending covert agents into 'chat rooms, online social networks, or even real-space groups.' He also proposes that the Government make secret payments to so-called 'independent' credible voices to bolster the Government's messaging..."[72]

CONCLUSION

America is under threat. Whether through domestic policy, foreign policy, national security, or appointments, Barack Obama has tried to profoundly reshape the United States. The reshaping is in his own image—that of a left-wing ideologue who spent the majority of his adult years in an ivory tower. Unfortunately for us, time and time again, history shows us that ivory tower thinking does not work in the real world.

CHAPTER 3

UNDERSTANDING OBAMA'S CONTEMPT FOR YOUR AMERICA

*"If ever a time should come, when vain and aspiring men shall pos-
sess the highest seats in government, our country will stand in need
of its experienced patriots to prevent its ruin."*[1]

—SAMUEL ADAMS

Obama's determination to radically reshape America doesn't make sense
until you trace his path to the White House—beginning with his
affiliation with the "New Party" and its founders.

Obama was endorsed by the New Party in 1996 in his run for Illinois State Senate, which he won. It is abundantly apparent that Barack
Obama not only knew what the New Party was when he sought its
endorsement, but through his ties with ACORN, the radical Left
activist organization, and the Service Employees International Union
(SEIU), it was Obama's radical Left connections that got him elected
to the Illinois State Senate.

"NEW PARTY" HISTORY

Most of the New Party's history has been lost in the digital age. The party was established in 1992 and started to die out in 1998, well before Google and the modern web were established. But through lengthy searches of the Nexis archive and microfilm, a disturbing picture emerges.

The New Party was established in 1992 "by union activist Sandy Pope and University of Wisconsin professor Joel Rogers," *USA Today* reported on November 16, 1992. The paper wrote that the new party was "self-described [as] 'socialist democratic.'"

The New Party was a loose confederation of unions, socialists, Communists, and black activists who shared common values, but often had different goals. Its party platform included:

- full employment
- a shorter work week
- guaranteed minimum income for all adults and a universal "social wage"
- full public financing of elections with universal voter registration
- "the democratization of banking and financial systems," which included public control and regulation of banking
- a more progressive tax system
- reductions in military spending and an end to unilateral military interventions.

Throughout its creation and rise, the New Party sought to unite alienated leftists who had grown disgusted by Bill Clinton's embrace of the center-left Democratic Leadership Council. The *Wisconsin State Journal* summed up where the Left was in February 1992. "Angry Americans," Jesse Waldman wrote, "particularly left-wing Democrats, are tired of choosing between the lesser of two evils when they go to the ballot now." A July 4, 1996, column in the *Los Angeles Times* by Todd Gitlin, which championed the New Party as "both old-fashioned and elegant," proclaimed the New Party as a path to victory for leftists alienated by the Democrats and Republicans. Capturing the mood of the Left in a May 31, 1998, article for the leftist magazine *In These Times*, Doug Ireland wrote, "As Bob Master of the Communication Workers of America—the point-man for the new labor ballot line— puts it: 'The political perspective of labor and working people has no voice in state politics, especially since the Democratic Party has moved to the right.'"

The seeds, however, had been sown all the way back in 1988. Quoting John Nichols in the March 22, 1998, issue of *In These Times*, "The roots of the New Party go back to the aftermath of Jesse Jackson's run for president in 1988.   At that time, Dan Cantor, who had served as labor coordinator for the Jackson campaign, and University of Wisconsin sociology professor Joel Rogers began talking about how to formulate an alternative between the increasingly indistinguishable Democratic-Republican monolith."

It is no great leap to say, as a result, that Barack Obama's rise to the Democratic nomination is the child of Jesse Jackson's defeat.

Fusion

In light of dissatisfaction with the Democrats' rightward drift, the New Party set about establishing itself as a third party for ballot access. "Fusion," was the idea. Continuing with Jesse Waldman from the *Wisconsin State Journal*, "[Fusion] would allow a left-wing candidate... to run as both a Democrat and [a third party] candidate. Proponents of this 'fusion' strategy include Mary K. Baum, co-chair of Wisconsin Labor-Farm, and Joel Rogers, a UW-Madison law and sociology professor who has helped organize the New Party."

Fusion is a pretty simple concept. A candidate could run as both a Democrat and a New Party member to signal—like Obama—he was, in fact, a left-leaning candidate. If the candidate received only 500 votes in the Democratic Party against another Democratic candidate who received 1,000 votes, he would clearly not be the nominee. But, if he also received 600 votes from the New Party, the New Party votes and Democratic votes would be fused. He would be the Democratic nominee with 1,100 votes.

The fusion idea set off a number of third parties, but the New Party was probably the most successful. A March 22, 1998, *In These Times* article by John Nichols showed just how successful. "[The *Wall Street*] *Journal*'s editorialists fretted last fall about how the New Party was responsible for a labor movement that was drifting leftward.... As [openly declared socialist] Rep. Bernie Sanders (I-Vt.) puts it, 'If the *Wall Street Journal* editorial page goes after you, you can pretty well bet you're doing the right thing.'"[2]

Fusion, fortunately for the country, died in 1997. William Rehnquist, writing for a 6–3 Supreme Court, found the concept was not a protected constitutional right, despite arguments from left-wing interest groups. It was two years too late to stop Obama.[3]

OBAMA, ACORN, AND THE NEW PARTY

Barack Obama could not have been elected without his affiliation with ACORN. As Stanley Kurtz reported, "Acorn is the key modern successor of the radical 1960's 'New Left,' with a '1960's-bred agenda of anti-capitalism' to match."[4] And Barack Obama was ACORN's lawyer.

Using his position at ACORN in 1995, Obama set up the playing field for his election in 1996. *The Boston Globe* reports, "Obama was part of a team of attorneys who represented the Association of Community Organizations for Reform Now (ACORN) in a lawsuit against the state of Illinois in 1995 for failing to implement a federal law designed to make it easier for the poor and others to register as voters.

A federal court ordered the state to implement the law." The *Globe* also notes, "Obama was part of a team of lawyers representing black voters and aldermen that forced Chicago to redraw ward boundaries that the City Council drew up after the 1990 census. They said the boundaries were discriminatory. After an appeals court ruled the map violated the federal Voting Rights Act, attorneys for both sides drew up a new set of ward boundaries."

With districts redrawn (ingratiating him to black politicians on his side of the city) and rules loosened on voter registration, Obama could move on to higher office. Obama sought the New Party endorsement, which required him to sign a contract that he would keep up his relationship with the New Party.

Using ACORN's get-out-the-vote efforts and relying on his gerrymandered Democrat district, Obama moved on to the State Senate. While there, he paid back the New Party and the far Left. He opposed the Born Alive Infant Protection act, he opposed legislation that would have prohibited the sale of pornography across the street from elementary schools and churches, and he supported allowing criminals to sue their victims if their victims injured the criminals in self-defense.

Beyond a shadow of a doubt, Barack Obama knew what he was getting into, and he remains an ideal New Party candidate. The New Party was, and as it still exists is, an amalgamation of the Left and far Left designed to attract far Left candidates and move the Democratic Party back to the Left. Barack Obama is an example of the New Party's success.

THE ALINSKY CONNECTION

To understand the current president of the United States, what he believes, and where he might lead us, there is another critical dimension to the Obama education which we must consider carefully. It is the influence of radical Saul Alinsky, and his *Rules for Radicals*, on

Barack Obama. Perhaps no one has stated it more clearly and incisively than Paul Sperry (a Hoover Institution Media Fellow and former *Investors Business Daily* Washington Bureau Chief) in his recent article in *Investors Business Daily* entitled "Alinsky's Star Pupil Uses 'Rules' As a Manual for Social Surgery:"

Alinsky's Star Pupil Uses 'Rules' As A Manual For 'Social Surgery'

By PAUL SPERRY

President Obama is fond of using ridicule to frustrate critics. He recently mocked Republicans for predicting "Armageddon" if healthcare reform passed. After signing the bill, he cracked that he looked around to "see if there were any asteroids falling," only to discover a nice day with "birds chirping."

Obama has also used the tactic to dismiss charges that he's pushing a "socialist" agenda, arguing that critics will next accuse him of "being a secret communist because I shared my toys in kindergarten."

But the former community organizer also knows that ridiculing the opposition is an effective tactic taught by the father of community organizing, Saul D. Alinsky—a socialist agitator from Chicago whose influence on Obama is deeper than commonly known.

In fact, the tactic is ripped right from the pages of "Rules for Radicals" (Vintage Books, New York, 1971), a how-to manual Alinsky wrote for coat-and-tie revolutionaries.

"Ridicule is man's most potent weapon," reads Rule No. 5. "It is almost impossible to counterattack ridicule. Also it infuriates the opposition, who then react to your advantage."

It's just one of 13 rules Alinsky coached his acolytes to follow to "take power away from the Haves." The Haves, represented foremost by corporate America, are "the enemy."
They must be identified, singled out and targeted for attack—
and the more personal the better, Alinsky advised, putting a
special bull's-eye on banks.

His 13th rule—"Pick the target, freeze it, personalize it and
polarize it"—is not lost on Obama, who has targeted "fat
cat" bankers, "predatory" lenders, "greedy" insurers and
industrial "polluters" as enemies of the people.

"Obama learned his lesson well," said David Alinsky, son
of the late socialist. "I am proud to see that my father's model
for organizing is being applied successfully beyond local community organizing."

Obama first learned Alinsky's rules in the 1980s, when
Alinskyite radicals with the Chicago-based Alinsky group
Gamaliel Foundation recruited, hired, trained and paid him
as a community organizer in South Side Chicago.

They also helped him get into Harvard Law School to
"learn power's currency in all its intricacy and detail," as
Obama put it in his memoir. A Gamaliel board member even
wrote a letter of recommendation for him.

Obama took a break from his Harvard studies to travel to
Los Angeles for eight days of intense training at Alinsky's
Industrial Areas Foundation, a station of the cross for
acolytes. In turn, he trained other community organizers in
Alinsky agitation tactics. In 1988, he even wrote a chapter for
the book "After Alinsky: Community Organizing in Illinois,"
in which he lamented organizers' "lack of power" in implementing change.

Decades later, power would no longer be an issue, as Obama infiltrated the highest echelons of the political establishment, thus fulfilling Alinsky's vision of a new "vanguard" of coat-and-tie radicals sneaking behind enemy lines. He preached that changing the system "means working in the system"—while not acting or looking radical. "Start them easy," he said in his book, "don't scare them off."

It worked like a charm for Obama. And during the presidential campaign, he hired one of his Gamaliel mentors, Mike Kruglik, to train young campaign workers in Alinsky tactics at "Camp Obama," a school set up at Obama headquarters in Chicago. The tactics helped Obama capture the youth vote like no other president before him.

After the election, his other Gamaliel mentor, Jerry Kellman (who actually hired him and whose identity Obama disguised in his memoir), helped the Obama administration establish Organizing for America, which mobilizes young supporters to agitate for Obama's legislative agenda using "Rules for Radicals"—which Alinsky dedicated to "Lucifer, the very first radical known to man who rebelled against the establishment and did it so effectively that he at least won his own kingdom."

In fact, the 1971 book, now selling well on Amazon, is required reading for students applying for the program.

"Rules" is more than a manual. It's a diary of Alinsky's worldview, a dark, anti-capitalist one made all the more disturbing knowing that his protege sits in the Oval Office, where he's systematically reorganizing our economy, one industry at a time.

A careful reading of Alinsky's 200-page book leaves you queasy. Even before you get to his rules, which start on Page 126, you realize he hates everything dear to Americans while respecting nothing sacred about America—even its founding. He ridicules our most basic morality. He mocks our founders, finding the worst even in Jefferson, a classical liberal.

Alinsky, who died of a heart attack at 63, valued democracy merely as a "means" toward achieving "economic justice." He laughed at "middle class moral hygiene." He even rebuked activists burdened by decency and troubled by the ethics of his tactics, sneering that they would rather go home with their "ethical hymen intact" than win a battle at any cost.

Alinsky was more than a socialist. He was a moral anarchist. Listen to these perverse proverbs:

- "Ethical standards must be elastic."
- "In war the end justifies almost any means."
- "In a fight almost anything goes."
- "It is a world not of angels but of angles."
- "The real arena is corrupt."
- "'Reconciliation' means that when one side gets the power and the other side gets reconciled to it, then we have reconciliation." (GOP lawmakers take note.)
- "All values are relative."

Bitterly contemptuous of American materialism and individualism, Alinsky was a big fan of Lenin, whom he called a "pragmatist." He claimed that his own philosophy was anchored in "hope" for a more just world.

But this privileged son was simply bored with the status quo and sought to smash it just to see it smashed, while masquerading his unprincipled pique as an altruistic crusade for the downtrodden.

"Agitate," he egged on fellow radicals, "create disenchantment and discontent with the current values," even if none exist.

His story is similar to that of unrepentant terrorist Bill Ayers, the rebellious son of a successful Chicago businessman. Alinsky's father owned his own business in the city and put his son through the University of Chicago studying archeology.

Alinsky comes across loud and clear in the narrative of "Rules for Radicals" as a bitter, vulgar Hobbesian cynic. He advocates "fart-ins" and "sh**-ins" to offend the establishment, explaining that the "one thing" that inner-city organizers want to do to whites is "sh** on them." Nothing is off limits. The only thing he truly romanticizes is "ego."

"The ego of the organizer is stronger and more monumental than the ego of the leader," he wrote. "The organizer is in a true sense reaching for the highest level for which man can reach...to play God." He added: "Ego must be so all-pervading that the personality of the organizer is contagious."

Page 23 of "Rules" is chilling: The American individualist—the industrialist, the entrepreneur, the wealth creator—"is beginning to learn that he will either share part of his material wealth or lose all of it; that he will respect and learn to live with other political ideologies"—that is, neo-Marxism—"if he wants civilization to go on."

"If he does not share his bread, he dare not sleep, for his neighbor will kill him," Alinsky warned. In other words, sacrifice and pay your fair share for "social justice" (code for socialism) or face mass unrest and the anger of the mob. Anarchy. Chaos. Blood in the streets.

Alinsky describes "the Haves" of American society as having fallen "asleep"—ripe for slaughter. "It is as though the great law of change had prepared the anesthetization of the victim prior to the social surgery to come."

Is Obama acting as Alinsky's star social surgeon, the first to possess the necessary power to carve up the American economy for mass redistribution? If so, "Rules for Radicals" may be his operating manual. More of us should read it.

For those who voted for Obama for President, Sperry may have highlighted more "change" than they bargained for.

CHAPTER 4

REBELLION: AMERICA'S BIRTHRIGHT

We stand at once the wonder and admiration of the whole world, and we must enquire what it is that has given us so much prosperity. This cause is that every man can make himself.[1]

—ABRAHAM LINCOLN

It didn't start with Obama, or the Democrats, or even big-government Republicans who have helped them. Despite our nation being founded out of a rebellion over taxes, with the cry, "Taxation without representation is tyranny,"[2] we've been saddled with more tyranny than what we threw off. England's taxation of the colonies was paltry compared to our current tax load.

When our nation was founded, the federal government spent the equivalent of about $3 million a year—about $1 per person.[3] By 1910, after 120 years of operation, our federal government spent just over $600 million—about $6.75 per person.[4] (There had been modest inflation in the intervening years.) But that's pocket change compared to today. By contrast, now the federal government spends $10 billion *every day* (almost $12,000 per person per year).[5] How did this come to pass?

Prior to 1913, "under the Constitution, Congress could impose direct taxes only if they were levied in proportion to each state's population. Thus, when a flat rate Federal income tax was enacted in 1894, it was quickly challenged, and in 1895, the U.S. Supreme Court ruled it unconstitutional because it was a direct tax not apportioned according to the population of each state."[6]

That changed with the adoption of the Sixteenth Amendment, which allowed a federal income tax to be imposed as a direct tax, unapportioned to the states. As a result, Federal spending as a percentage of Gross Domestic Product (GDP) has grown from 3 percent to about 25 percent.[7]

Taxation *with representation* has turned into a nightmare. Government is the "senior partner" in every American business, and its tax burden is the largest item in every working American's budget. Americans pay more for "being governed" than for food, clothing, and shelter combined. In 1929—the last year before massive federal expansion under Franklin Delano Roosevelt—federal, state, and local taxes equaled about 10 percent of our GDP.[8] Today, combined taxes are over 26 percent of the economic earnings, but because governments are running such huge deficits, there is another 12 percent of our economy that the government is spending, which is essentially "deferred taxes" imposed on the next generation of young Americans. Total "current" plus "deferred" taxes were about 38 percent of the economy in 2009.

High taxes are not the price we pay for a free society; they are a threat to a free society and personal liberty. The condition that distinguishes a free man from a slave is dominion over himself and the fruits of his labor. Every dollar transferred through taxes takes power from the taxpaying citizen and gives it to the government.

DEMAGOGING TAX INCREASES

Despite an already heavy tax burden, Americans are continually under threat of increased taxes to feed the ravaging federal monster. Thanks to the policies and arguments of Ronald Reagan, taxpayer groups, fiscal conservatives in Congress, and new tea partiers, resistance to further increases has spread.

President Obama came to office promising no new taxes on Americans with incomes less than $250,000, but he promptly broke that promise in early 2009 as he raised taxes on cigarette consumers.[9] Politicians (especially Democrats) always demonize groups before hitting them with taxes, but cigarette consumers are just average folks, often with modest income, and they can't support all of Obama's spending. Consequently, Democrats also demonize the so-called "rich," targeting them for income tax increases. A huge share of income at the top end is actually small business income. Thus tax increases on the "rich" really just kill jobs for average Americans.

In 2006, 27 million individuals reported an estimated $938 billion in income from sole proprietorships, corporations, and partnerships on their tax returns (including capital gains passed through on Schedule D) and paid an estimated $159 billion in income taxes. (For comparison, it is estimated that, C corporations in 2006 paid $359 billion of corporate income tax, which implies net income of approximately $1,200 billion.)[10] In other words, according to the Department of Treasury, 75 percent of taxpayers in the top bracket are "flow-through" business owners, i.e., small businesses, sole proprietorships, freelance consultants, etc.

Obama and other liberals would like you to believe that high-income earners in the United States are under-taxed and do not pay their "fair share." Obama's campaign promise was that he would increase taxes on couples earning more than $250,000 per year and give tax breaks to those earning less. The reality is that the top 1 percent of taxpayers already pays almost 40 percent of all personal income taxes, and that share has nearly doubled over the last quarter-century.[11] Meanwhile, the bottom 50 percent of taxpayers pay less than 5 percent of federal personal income taxes.[12]

Though Democrats talk of shifting taxes to corporations and the wealthy to help low- and moderate-income familes, the truth is we have already shifted much of the tax burden to the wealthy. It is middle-income Americans who continue to pay the bulk of federal taxes.

Shifting taxes to corporations is a fantasy. Businesses do not pay taxes; only people pay them. An increase in corporate income tax, for example, is paid by customers in the form of increased prices, employees in the form of lower wages and shareholders in decreased dividends. So we the people pay for the tax increase, but the politicians like it because the taxes are rendered less visible to us.

In 1984, Americans were sold a tax increase that was advertised as a "down payment on the deficit." Remember? The politicians, however, used the new revenues not to reduce the deficit but to accommodate greater spending. Fiscal year 1985 saw one of the greatest increases of spending in our history—from $852 to $946 billion—more than an 11 percent increase.

This is an historic example of the fact that it's not tax cuts but dramatic spending increases that have caused our deficits. Tax reductions have merely offset tax-bracket creep.

Recently, total federal taxes have been inching up from 18 percent of GDP to about 19 percent. Spending has zoomed to over 25 percent of GDP.[13] Bailouts, "stimulus," and other uncontrolled spending have caused huge deficits.

Consider the fiscal problems of European countries such as Greece, Britain, and Spain these days. They have massive and growing piles of government debt even larger than our own (although we are heading in that direction). Yet every European country has income and payroll taxes, as we do, plus a Value Added Tax (VAT) that rakes in even more cash for the government. The average VAT rate in Europe—20 percent!—means that every purchase a European citizen makes hands a chunk of change over to the government, making everything at least 20 percent more expensive.[14] History confirms that high taxes don't solve a deficit problem; they just encourage politicians to spend more money.

As Brutus, the Anti-Federalist writing during the debates on ratifying the Constitution, warned:

> The power to tax, exercised without limitation, will introduce itself into every corner of the city, and country—it will enter the house of every gentleman, watch over his cellar, wait upon his cook in the kitchen, follow the servants into the parlor, preside over the table, and note down all he eats and drinks; it will take cognizance of the professional man in his office, or study; it will watch the merchant in the counting house, or any store; it will follow the mechanic to his shop, and in his work, and will haunt him in his family, and in his bed; it will be a constant companion of the industrious farmer in all his labor... it will penetrate into the most obscure cottage; and finally it will light upon the head of every person in the United States. To all these different classes of people, and in all these circumstances, in which it will attend them, the language in which it will address them, will be GIVE, GIVE.[15]

OTHER TAXES

In addition to income taxes, the government takes in money through Social Security taxes. Social Security taxes are second only to personal income taxes as the federal government's largest single source of revenue. Middle- and lower-income workers bear, proportionately, the greater share of Social Security taxes.[16]

Piled atop the personal income tax and Social Security taxes are federal corporation taxes, capital gains taxes, gasoline taxes, "luxury" taxes, liquor taxes, tobacco taxes, and a host of excises, customs, tariffs, licenses, and other fees. Most of these taxes are paid by the average American—often when they don't even know it.

Corporations, for example, are often favorite targets for politicians looking for some money. But businesses, whether large or small, don't pay taxes—they just collect them. The "taxes" that businesses supposedly pay are recouped in lower dividends to stockholders, lower wages for employees, and high prices for their customers. Politicians try to fool us into thinking "greedy business people" will pay, but the taxes fall on all of us in the form of incomes that are lower and prices that are higher than they would be without the taxes.

The tax burden of each American held relatively constant from our founding until the Civil War, and at a slightly higher but constant plateau until passage of the income tax (Sixteenth) amendment in 1913.[17] When the potential of the income tax became a reality in Washington, the individual tax burden grew by leaps and bounds.

CHAPTER 5

OUR NATION DERAILED

I ... place economy among the first and most important of republican virtues, and public debt as the greatest dangers to be feared. ... And to preserve (our) independence, we must not let our rulers load us with perpetual debt. We must make our election between economy and liberty, or profusion and servitude.[1]

—THOMAS JEFFERSON

Our government, as befits a free people, used to be the smallest and least meddlesome in any modern country. But now it has become everything that Jefferson feared: a spendthrift leviathan that squanders our labor and loads us with a mountainous public debt. Over the last half-century, no matter the party in power, our government has confiscated a greater and greater share of our national productivity. As public spending increases, personal freedom shrinks. We Americans, thinking ourselves still free, actually must work longer each year to pay for our government than the medieval serfs had to work for their feudal lords!

Just how we've come to be in this fiscal fix is a mystery to most Americans. And certainly it should be. When at least three-quarters of the people find deficits totally distasteful, how can they continue? To find the answer, we must review a little history.

GOVERNMENT BLOAT

Previously we discussed the key role of the Sixteenth Amendment in changing Washington's access to the pocketbooks of American tax-payers. Equally as important was the unwritten but solemnly honored rule of America's first 150 years that while the nation might run deficits during war-time, the debt should be retired during the ensuing peace. This methodology prevailed through the 1920s as the debt of World War I was being retired. Only as we endured the Great Depression was this unwritten constitutional rule against deficits ruptured, when people bought the argument that the government spending money was the answer to the nation's economic woes. Soon, deficit spending—borrowing and spending someone else's money (currently the Chinese)—was the answer to all sorts of government-identified maladies.

At the same time that commonly accepted financial wisdom was being chucked in the 1930s, the scope of federal activities became virtually limitless. A series of U.S. Supreme Court decisions eroded the time-honored constitutional barriers against federal encroachment into areas of human activity historically reserved to states, local government, private individuals, and private organizations. Congress happily took advantage by creating a blizzard of alphabet-soup programs and agencies to manage more aspects of America life.

The Supreme Court's decision in *Wickard* v. *Filburn* is a perfect encapsulation of the explosion of federal powers that occurred in the 1940s.[2] In *Wickard*, a farmer, Roscoe Filburn, grew wheat for personal use. The wheat was not sold to anyone. The federal government, intent on driving up the price of wheat, had imposed restrictions on how much wheat could be grown by farmers on their own land. Filburn exceeded the limits by growing some wheat to feed his livestock. The government's argument, that the Supreme Court ultimately bought, was that Filburn would have purchased wheat if he was not growing his own. In other words, after *Wickard*, the federal government had the power to restrict a person's use of his private property to grow his own food for his own use. If the federal government has that power, it has nearly unlimited power.

The crescendo of expansionist legal Gnosticism came full circle during the 2010 confirmation hearings of then Solicitor General Elena Kagan. Senator Tom Coburn (R-OK) asked a simple question: "If I wanted to sponsor a bill, and it said, 'Americans, you have to eat three vegetables and three fruits—every day.' And I got it through Congress and it's now the law of the land. Gotta do it. Does that violate the commerce clause?...Do we have the power to tell people what they have to eat every day?" Elena Kagan's answer? "Senator Coburn... I...it's...uh..."[3]

WITHHOLDING TAX—INTEREST-FREE LOANS TO THE GOVERNMENT

As the personal income tax began to reach into the pocket books of middle America, there was a practical limit to the amount that could be extracted from most working people at tax time every year. In 1944, the big spenders invented tax withholding, thereby making employers into federal tax collectors. This reduced the pain of the income tax on the theory that you won't miss what you never receive.

The withholding schedules have been designed to "over-withhold," qualifying most taxpayers for a refund. The psychology of April 15 has been converted from universal agony to a second Christmas for a sizable percentage of taxpayers who eagerly await their tax refunds.

So instead of encouraging individual saving and investments which harness the power of compound interest to increase wealth, the government takes more than what most taxpayers owe and then returns it without paying any interest.

So many Americans get a refund, they fail to realize both what they could have done with that extra money had the government not taken it in the first place (and then returned it interest-free), and just how much comes out of their pockets to begin with.

Of course, one of the greatest enablers of big government is the progressive nature of the income tax rate structure—also known as bracket creep. As average incomes increase, taxpayers are pushed into ever higher tax brackets. This in turn gives Congress a greater share of the national income without ever having to vote to raise taxes. With money pouring into the U.S. Treasury, Washington finds exciting new ways to spend it.

CONGRESS UNLEASHED

One of Washington's favorite ways to spend taxpayers' money is on itself. Consequently, Washington, D.C., has undergone a transformation of incredible proportions. From a tranquil southern town that "consumed" about 3 percent of the national income, it has burgeoned to become the "center of empire," à la Rome, that controls about one quarter of what we Americans produce each year.

The Departments of Navy, State, and War (housing the entire military command structure of the United States), comfortably shared one building in 1886, when the Eisenhower Executive Office Building (EEOB) was constructed. Located opposite the West Wing of the White House at the corner of 17th Street and Pennsylvania Avenue, the EEOB is now not even large enough to provide enough offices for all who serve on the president's staff.

Until the early years of the last century, senators and representatives had no offices (the first Senate and House office buildings were completed in 1908); they did their work in the House or Senate chambers, in committee hearings, or in the lobbies within the Capitol building itself.[4] They were paid $5,000 a year and regularly engaged in gainful employment back home.[5] And their staffs were small. There were only seventy personal staff members for ninety-six senators. This means that some senators had no staff at all. In 1914, the personal staff, plus the staff of the standing committees in both the House and Senate, totaled fewer than 400 people to serve the 531 members of the House and Senate.[6]

Big government took root during the Wilsonian era, matured during the New Deal, went on a rampage with Lyndon Johnson's "War on Poverty," and is now exploding under Obama. Congress's own budget illustrates this explosive growth in spending. In 1914, the cost of operating Congress was $7.5 million,[7] 7.5 cents per U.S. citizen. That cost has risen to $5.4 billion in 2010—$18 for every one of us in our nation—just to operate a Congress that has only four more members than it did in 1914. Or to look at it another way: each senator and representative costs taxpayers $14,000 for the entire year of 1914; in 2010 that annual cost had risen to over $10 million.

YEAR	CONGRESSIONAL BUDGET	COST TO EACH CITIZEN	COST OF SUPPORT FOR EACH MEMBER
1914	$7.5 million	$07.5	$14,000
2010	$5.4 billion	$18.00	$10 million

PERKS GALORE

The part-time "public service" contemplated by our Founding Fathers has been supplanted by full-time, career-oriented representatives and senators who, by and large, reside in Washington. They enjoy ever-increasing salaries. They are entitled to "franked" (postage-free) mail designed to keep senators' and representatives' names before their constituents. Other "perks" available to members of Congress include various free medical services, free gym facilities, free parking in Capitol garages and at local area airports, numerous free trips—the list goes on and on. Their pension system is among the most generous in the nation, allowing many congressmen to receive not only much more than they've paid in, but more per year than their current annual salary.[8]

Staff support is another perk the founders never envisioned. From the turn of the century, when senators and representatives had no private offices and few staffers, Congress now occupies six huge office buildings (and other peripheral buildings) and surrounds each senator with about forty personal staff, and each representative with approximately twenty. The House alone has approximately 10,000 personal staffers, including district office workers.[9]

There are also 3,000 or more committee leadership staff. Institutional staff (police, legislative clerks, janitorial workers, and majority and minority party floor staff) exceed 5,000. The Congressional Budget Office, General Accounting Office, and Library of Congress add another 8,000 or so.[10]

Then there's the matter of salary. Nearly 2,000 House staff members (20 percent) earn more than $100,000 a year, with forty-three of them earning the maximum: $172,500 per year.[11] Not bad for government work . . . and far in excess of most private-sector salaries.[12]

An increase in the number of staff has meant an increase in the quantity of legislation, fulfilling the promise that "work will fill the time available." Members rely almost entirely on their staff for policy decisions. Because of the virtually unlimited scope of Congress's activities, and the workload it has generated, staff members are the gears that keep the legislative branch humming.

As Mark Brisnow, a veteran staffer to three senators, three congressmen, and three different committees, confessed:

When I arrived on Capitol Hill as a junior aide for Senator

Hubert Humphrey in 1975, the Watergate scandal had con-
vinced congressmen that they needed to "assert" themselves
against the Imperial Presidency. How? By hiring more staff,
naturally. I came to learn there are all sorts of ways congressional staffers serve themselves or their bosses but not always
the national interest.... Congress has no less than 150 sub-
committees, and each one has its own staff that must justify
its existence. Many staffers draft bills just to raise a congressman's profile—and attract contributions from special interest
groups. Many of these bills have absolutely no chance of passing.... But aren't staffers essential to helping congressmen
comprehend the increasingly complex and broad-ranging
issues that they face? One might guess so, but actually lawmakers use staffers as a crutch. Why should a congressman
master a subject if an aide can do it for him? Just watch senators step out of the elevator on their way into the chamber
for a vote. Many will quickly glance to the side where aides
stand, compressing into a single gesture the sum of information their bosses need: thumbs up or thumbs down.[13]

Congressional bureaucracy has become as much a reality as executive
branch bureaucracy. Much of the time of the legislative bureaucracy
is devoted to so-called "constituent service," acting as ombudsmen for
a constituent who might be confronted with seemingly intractable
problems with a department or agency. Ironically, Congress has generated this workload for itself over the years by having created the very
departments, agencies, and programs with which it now must cope.

"There are now signs that the limits of capacity have been
reached.... The enormous extension of the activities of the federal
government generates a volume of detailed and complex business
which I believe has gone beyond the capacity of Congress to handle.... A law of diminishing returns is actively at work in the field of

the federal government.... The workload is beyond effective legislative control." [14] A lamentation of a member in 2010? No—testimony on the Legislative Reorganization Act in 1948. Even then it was apparent to many that Washington was simply trying to do too much, and that the federal government was out of control.

The federal government has grown so large that no single individual can possibly comprehend it in any kind of detail. Senators and members of Congress will acknowledge that while they might master the governmental activities controlled by the committees on which they serve, it is impossible to be conversant with everything government does. There is simply no one in charge.

Since those whom we elect are overwhelmed, the non-elected take over. The bureaucrats and congressional staff really manage the government—and as often as not, they do it their way. And the sheer size of the government behemoth serves to obscure their transgressions. Even worse, many congressional staffers are more interested in resume-building on their way to comfy lobbyist and trade association jobs than they are on the actual constitutionality of what they do.

Beyond the size of government per se, we have simply asked the federal government to do too many different kinds of things, and it is doing none of them well. Those elected to the federal government must comprehend and administer all areas of human existence. As a result, the things which only the federal government can do—defense, foreign affairs, national security—suffer as our president and key congressional leaders spend their limited time on everything from roads to welfare to food stamps, student loans, sewer systems, anthropological studies, cancer research, air traffic control, weather prediction, land management, dredging harbors, preserving Indian lore, building jet fighters, staffing embassies, preventing terrorism, protecting farmers, regulating financial institutions, cleaning up after hurricanes and oil spills, controlling communication, putting up satellites, regulating highway speed, and determining the acceptable miles-per-gallon of our automobiles. This is only a tiny peek at the range of human concerns with which Washington deals.

Congress tries to cope with the proliferation of responsibilities through committees and sub-committees, giving chairmen enormous powers. The committee system is a perfectly logical and manageable approach, so long as each legislator has a chance to assess and reflect upon the recommendations of the committee.

But when everyone is so "stretched" that the committee recommendations are not adequately tested and challenged, the nation's policy is determined largely by committees (and, increasingly, by their non-elected staffs) and by the chairmen who accede to power—not by any particular measure of competence, but primarily by seniority (and in the House, by the degree of loyalty exhibited toward the party). Those things which only the federal government can and must do compete for time and attention with things that states, local governments, and private individuals and organizations can (and should) do, leaving true national priorities to suffer.

Stretched as it is to handle its legitimate workload, Congress should not be "showboating" with hearings and probes designed to pillory and skewer the political opponents of those in charge of Congress. Yet, consider Henry Waxman summoning corporate executives from tobacco company CEOs to insurance CEOs who, after the passage of ObamaCare, issued notices of increased healthcare costs and set up reserves to cover the new costs. (Because of various SEC regulations and laws, if a corporation fails to disclose increased costs it has reason to know about, the CEO of the company can be punished.) In a damned-if-you-do, damned-if-you-don't situation, Congressman Waxman demanded the CEOs of these corporations appear before Congress to answer for their actions. Only after Republicans loudly protested did Waxman back down.[15]

But it is not just Waxman. Republican Senator John McCain and others have held hearings on such pressing issues as steroids in professional sports (possibly to leverage the NCAA to scrap its BCS system for college football). The ability of an unrestrained Congress to grand-stand on C-SPAN creates a dangerous incursion into citizen freedom.

While there can be little dispute that C-SPAN cameras and other news media coverage of Congress have contributed to heightened transparency for the American public, there is also a more sinister side—the ability of members of Congress to launch show trials and witch hunts. It is time that Congress imposed some self-restraint and limited itself to the people's business—which the Founders actually took the time to elucidate in the Constitution. In Article I, Section 8, they expressly limited Congress to eighteen powers:

1. The Congress shall have Power To lay and collect Taxes. Duties, imposts and Excises, to pay the Debts and provide for the common Defence and general Welfare of the United States; but all Duties, imposts and Excises shall be uniform through the United States;
2. To borrow Money on the credit of the United States;
3. To regulate Commerce with foreign Nations, and among the several States, and with the Indian Tribes;
4. To establish an uniform Rule of Naturalization, and uni-form Laws on the subject of Bankruptcies throughout the United States;
5. To coin Money, regulate the Value thereof, and of foreign Coin, and fix the Standard of Weights and Measures;
6. To provide for the Punishment of counterfeiting the Secu-rities and current Coin of the United States;
7. To establish Post Offices and post Roads;
8. To promote the Progress of Science and useful Arts, by securing for limited Times to Authors and Inventors the exclusive Right to their respective Writings and Discoveries;
9. To constitute Tribunals inferior to the supreme Court;

10. To define and punish Piracies and Felonies committed on the high Seas, and Offences against the Law of Nations;

11. To declare War, grant Letters of Marque and Reprisal, and make Rules concerning Captures on Land and Water;

12. To raise and support Armies, but no Appropriation of Money to that Use shall be for a longer Term than two Years;

13. To provide and maintain a Navy;

14. To make Rules for the Government and Regulation of the land and naval Forces;

15. To provide for calling forth the Militia to execute the Laws of the Union, suppress Insurrections and repel Invasions;

16. To provide for organizing, arming, and disciplining, the Militia, and for governing such Part of them as may be employed in the Service of the United States, reserving to the States respectively, the Appointment of the Officers, and the Authority of training the Militia according to the discipline prescribed by Congress;

17. To exercise exclusive Legislation in all Cases whatsoever, over such District (not exceeding ten Miles square) as may, by Cession of particular States, and the Acceptance of Congress, become the Seat of the Government of the United States, and to exercise like Authority over all Places purchased by the Consent of the Legislature of the State in which the Same shall be, for the Erection of Forts, Magazines, Arsenals, dock-Yards, and other needful Buildings;—And

18. To make all Laws which shall be necessary and proper for carrying into Execution the foregoing Powers, and all other Powers vested by this Constitution in the Government of the United States, or in any Department or Officer thereof.

Note what is NOT included as federal functions and responsibilities:

- Any reference to education or a Department of Education. That was always meant to be a private, religious or state and local public responsibility.
- Any reference to agriculture or a Department of Agriculture. That was always a private farmer/Farm Bureau/state and local agricultural commission responsibility.
- Any reference to labor or a Department of Labor.
- Any reference to energy or a Department of Energy. That was all private—and as power companies emerged, they were regulated by local and state governments, except for nuclear energy which had national defense implications and interstate power transmission.
- Any reference to transportation, other than "post roads," or a Department of Transportation. That was always private or state and local responsibility.
- Any reference to housing or a Department of Housing and Urban Development. That was always a private enterprise and very local/state function and relationship.

Small wonder the government is hemorrhaging money.

CHAPTER 6

BURIED UNDER A MOUNTAIN OF DEBT

I can scarcely contemplate a greater calamity that could befall this country, than be loaded with a debt exceeding their ability ever to discharge. If this be a just remark, it is unwise and improvident to vest in the general government a power to borrow at discretion, without any limitation or restriction.[1]

—BRUTUS, ANTI-FEDERALIST

Unless something drastic is done, our federal debt will hit 90 percent of our GDP within a decade or less.[2] Federal spending has already grossly exceeded tax receipts which will inevitably result in higher taxes to pay for it. On top of the $3.7 trillion Obama budget for just this year—2010—the unaccounted-for burden of ObamaCare will require trillions of additional dollars. America's finances have put us at risk of losing our high credit rating.[3]

When a nation's accumulated debt exceeds 90 percent of GDP, it has reached a "tipping point" with serious adverse effects on the rate of economic growth, reducing growth by as much as two points below what might otherwise have been.[4] We cannot afford to sacrifice economic growth at a time when our nation needs it most in order to manage the entitlement demands of the 78 million "baby boomers" on the brink of retirement.[5]

Obama's fiscal excesses have caused America's status on Heritage Foundation's "2010 Index of Economic Freedom" to implode. For the first time in the Index's sixteen years, the United States has dropped from an economically "free" country to "mostly free." As the Index reveals, lack of economic freedom has a direct, negative effect on job growth.[6]

UNDERSTANDING OUR NATIONAL DEBT

The national debt is much larger than it first appears because of the way the federal government keeps its books. Instead of going by accrual basis, which recognizes and accounts for transactions (revenues and expenditures) at the time they are incurred, the government uses a cash accounting basis. The accrual method would take into account the promises that we have made for future expenditures—to military and civilian retirees of the federal government, to Social Security and Medicare beneficiaries, and for other obligations the government has taken on.

Federal debt held by the public is our "cash" national debt. Because that's the debt we keep track of on the books of the United States government—the debt for which the Treasury Department issues T-bills and other debt instruments—it is the one we have to pay interest on each and every year to keep the federal government out of bankruptcy.

By the cash accounting basis, federal debt held by the public now stands at about $9.1 trillion, up from $7.5 trillion last year.[7] That represents a mortgage of about $77,000 for each household in the nation.[8] For fiscal year 2010, interest payments on the federal debt held by the public will exceed $200 billion.[9] However, the Congressional Budget Office's analysis of President Obama's 2011 budget proposal projects that the cost of paying interest by 2020 will be almost $1 trillion. As a percentage of GDP, this would equal to 4 percent of the economy consumed by interest payments alone.[10]

Large companies are required by federal law to go on the accrual basis. When you buy an insurance policy, or an annuity, or receive a private pension plan, there is a legal requirement that the company managers handling the funds invest and build the fund so it's there when you call upon it. If they don't do so, they can go to jail. If the same standards had been applied over the years to those in Congress who have voted for benefits but have failed to provide for raising the money necessary to fund them, we'd have generations of "public servants" behind bars.

HOW MUCH DO WE OWE?

There are various estimates of the dollar value of the accrued—or so-called "unfunded"—liabilities of the federal government—promised future payments that have not been funded. Social Security and Medicare have an unfunded liability currently estimated at $107 trillion.[11] In other words, the government would have to set aside $107 trillion today in order to meet our obligations to future retirees under current law.[12] Retirement obligations to federal civilian and military personnel, for which no investment has been provided, simply compound the problem.

As the number of workers declines relative to the number of people who have claims on the federal treasury, there is going to be a terrible crunch. And the politicians who launched these politically attractive but devastatingly costly obligations will all be dead and gone.

Between 1970 and 2010, the GDP grew from $4.7 trillion to $14.6 trillion in real terms. During the same period, the publicly held national debt grew from $1.6 trillion to $9.1 trillion. As a percentage of GDP, debt held by the public has grown from 28 percent to 64 percent.[13] As noted earlier, the most worrisome trend is the Congressional Budget Office projection that under President Obama's latest budget, the figure will be 90 percent of GDP by the end of 2020.[14]

It is the rapid, dramatic increases in spending that have exploded our national debt. Now the Obama Administration wants to raise taxes to attack the deficit. We know from experience that does not work. Tax increases, especially during a recession, are counterproductive to economic growth and recovery. The very talk of tax increases by this Administration, coupled with its clear disdain for free market job creators, has created uncertainty and exacerbated and lengthened the recession.

CHAPTER 7

INVASION OF THE MONEY SNATCHERS

> It is the highest impertinence and presumption...in kings and ministers, to pretend to watch over the economy of private people, and to restrain their expense, either by sumptuary laws, or by prohibiting the importation of foreign luxuries. They are themselves always, and without exception, the greatest spendthrifts in the society. Let them look well after their own expenses, and they may safely entrust private people with theirs. If their own extravagance does not ruin the state, that of their subjects never will.[1]
>
> —ADAM SMITH, *THE WEALTH OF NATIONS,* 1776

How did America transition from a very limited government to a virtually limitless federal structure that has driven taxes and spending to unprecedented levels? The "rest of the story" is found in an analysis of how representation really works—the dynamic interaction between those whom we elect and those whom our elected officials really end up representing.

Once the imposition of the income tax guaranteed a steady stream of federal revenue and the potential for using government as an instrument for coercive social change became apparent, social engineers looked to Washington. Much of the bad policy from the late twentieth and early twenty-first centuries can be traced back to the rise of the progressive movement in the early 1900s with a Republican named Robert LaFollette.

In 1891, LaFollette became Governor of Wisconsin and championed what he called the "Wisconsin Idea": technocrats could solve all the world's problems, and political nominations should be fought in primary elections instead of conventions or voter referenda efforts. LaFollette also supported the minimum wage and the income tax.[2]

Among the many dangerous ideas on which LaFollette pontificated and the American political class embraced was the idea of the professional, technocratic bureaucrat. By offloading the demands of governance to a permanent bureaucracy, both Congress and the president could shift blame to a nameless, faceless, permanent government class.

Those professional technocrats, secure in their jobs within a professional civil service protected from presidents who might want to fire them, became a welcoming home for academics and others who wanted to change society—the social engineers.

Social engineers were responsible for the explosion of government agencies in the 1930s. Using the economic woes of the time as their justification, they actually exacerbated many of the problems they sought to solve. Their programs and agencies began as fragile children, some of whom died in infancy at the hands of an initially unfriendly Supreme Court. But as the judicial climate changed, many of their expensive offspring grew to parasitic adulthood.

Since those uneasy beginnings, new programs and agencies have proliferated like mushrooms in a dark cave. And each one has become more adroit at survival and expansion. The sinister truth about government programs is that, regardless of whether they accomplish anything worthwhile, they build a constituency for their perpetuation. To paraphrase Will Rogers's comment that "I never met a man I didn't like," government responds, "I never saw a program I didn't want to keep."

An example of the development of a program that has enormous momentum is food stamps. Food stamps were first issued some forty years ago. Before then, they did not exist. There simply were no food stamps. The program started with a few million dollars and a handful of recipients; today food stamps are received by over 30 million people (one out of every ten people in the United States)[3] and cost tens of billions of dollars every year.[4]

Has the food stamp program eliminated hunger? Not if you listen to advocates for the poor. By the government's measure of poverty, the portion of the population that is below the so-called poverty line today is not substantially different from 1967. Why, then, does such a program continue? Because there are too many interests with stakes in them, including the Members of the House and Senate from farm states whose agriculture committees oversee the program; the Department of Agriculture's vast bureaucracy that administers the program; the suppliers to the program—farmers, storage and transportation companies, supermarket chains, the retail clerks union, as well as the farm lobbyists, agriculture trade groups, the social "public interest" groups, and the *recipients* of the stamps.

Think of the political "reach" of those interests. They are awesome. Despite many food stamp abuses, these special-interest groups have successfully resisted any significant reduction in the program. Americans prefer to believe federal departments and agencies are subject to the will of the president and Congress. If a program or department becomes outmoded, wasteful, duplicative, or just plain unnecessary, those whom we elect will get rid of it. Right? Hardly!

Bureaucracy has devised defense mechanisms that make pruning of government a very difficult task, indeed. The irony is that these defenses are paid for by us. Taxpayers' resources are employed to prevent the pruning. These defense mechanisms fall into the following categories:

■ Direct Lobbying—Despite the fact that federal law prohibits lobbying by federal employees, "legislative liaison" offices have emerged in every department and agency in order to "respond" to inquiries and requests from Congress. No one has been able to get a handle on the amount of money devoted to the salaries and activities of these offices, but clearly they amount to hundreds of millions of dollars. These bureaucracy liaison personnel are among the most prolific and persuasive in Washington, often "outshooting" the hired-gun lobbyists in the private sector. These advocates present and defend department and agency budgets and are often the source of new and expanded activities of their "employers." For, after all, the number of employees and budget size dictates the advancement, pay, and prestige of practically everyone in government.

■ Semi-direct Lobbying—Taxpayer funds are often granted to advocacy organizations that engage in direct lobbying of Congress on behalf of activities of the department or agency. These grants fund political conferences and grass-roots organizational activities, that, if successful, will generate an increasing demand for the "services" of that department or agency leading to an expansion of its budget. In the early days of the war on poverty, grants were often given to people to go door-to-door to work in community centers to expand the base of people eligible for welfare, housing assistance, food stamps, and other taxpayer-provided programs. The euphemism for all this activity in government circles is "outreach." What it really means is using your money to communicate the availability of more of your money.

■ Indirect Lobbying—Increasingly, government employees are members of employee associations or unions. A portion of your tax money that flows to pay the salaries of government employees is passed in the form of dues to organizations that lobby to increase the power and size of the federal government. Public-employee unions are the fastest growing unions in America, thanks to your tax dollars. The government-employee affiliates of the AFL-CIO and other public-employee unions lobby for a big spending social welfare agenda and contribute heavily to the liberal, big spending members of Congress who, in turn, seek to expand those activities which will create more dues-paying jobs.

Social-worker and teachers' organizations are dependent for their power on the "pass through" of taxes in the form of dues. When the poverty lawyers first came on the scene in the late 1960s and early 1970s, they saw a great opportunity to influence the mainstream legal profession. Using part of their taxpayer-provided salaries, the poverty lawyers paid dues to the National Legal Aid and Defenders Association (NLADA—part of the American Bar Association), and through sheer numbers took control of NLADA. Through it, they influenced the ABA to accept plaintiff solicitation and other case "manufacturing" techniques that had been considered unethical over the years.[5]

■ Informal Lobbying—In Washington, it is not at all uncommon for a wife to be employed in one department or agency while her husband works for a House or Senate member. The mere proximity of all the elements of the federal government assures a very high level of informal lobbying that, in many instances, is more effective than the work of those lobbyists who are registered or who populate the congressional liaison offices. The bureaucracy's skill at protecting its interests through lobbying of all types has created a virtual perpetual-motion machine of departments and agencies in Washington.

Perhaps no finer example of bureaucratic lobbying exists than Fannie Mae and Freddie Mac. Freddie and Fannie were recently placed under federal government conservatorship because of gross mismanagement and financial losses. Republicans in the United States Senate tried to ensure neither organization could continue their paid lobbying efforts, which amounted to a government agency hiring K Street lobbyists to lobby the government on behalf of government entities. Democrats blocked the efforts.

Over the years, the special-interest groups have become increasingly professional and capable. They have become adept not only at carving a *piece* of the government pie but at increasing the size of the pie. This is perfectly understandable. As more money has flowed to Washington to be spent, more able people have followed that money to influence how it is spent. One need only review the migration to Washington over the last half-century of various business, trade, and other special-interest organizations, as well as the proliferation of lobbyists and law firms, to know where the power in this country lies.

In the more than forty years since Lyndon Johnson's Great Society, lobbying firms and business, trade, public-interest, and other such organizations have multiplied dramatically. The number of such organizations headquartered in Washington and the Washington "Beltway" area has increased substantially, as has the relocation of the headquarters of large national companies. Washington's share of these organizations grew significantly, while New York and other areas of the nation have experienced a decrease in the number of associations headquartered outside Washington. Of the 7,600 national trade associations, approximately 2,000 of them are headquartered in the Washington area.

Even these figures do not tell the whole story. Many organizations that maintain their principal headquarters outside Washington have opened a Washington office or increased dramatically the size of existing Washington offices. National trade groups employ many people in Washington, making it the third-largest industry after government and tourism. Since the role of associations has increasingly turned to lobbying the government, what better place to do it than in Washington?[6]

GOVERNMENT LOBBIES GOVERNMENT

It is not surprising that private interests lobby Congress for special benefits and favors. However, the most rapid growth in lobbying and grant-seeking has been by state and local governments—and states have reaped the benefits. After Social Security and national defense, federal aid to states is the third-largest item in the budget. In just a decade and a half, aid programs for states have nearly doubled.[7]

Like moths gathering around the flame, the number of states that have hired Washington lobbyists has doubled over the past decade or so.[8] And the lobbyists actively seek out state and local government clients. So we, as both federal and state and local taxpayers, are taking a double hit—paying for lobbyists in Washington and driving up the size of federal programs by the demands our state and local lobbyists are placing on the system.

The only ones getting rich are the lobby firms. For example, the lobbying firm of Alcalde & Fay generates $4 million annually in fees from its "Municipalities Practice Group," charging their state and local clients retainers of $10,000 to $20,000 per month. They boast that they have secured billions of dollars in earmarked appropriations and federal grants.[9] Perhaps the most successful hired gun for the state and local governments is the Democrat lobbying shop of Cassidy & Associates. Gerald Cassidy, co-founder of the firm, cornered the earmarking process for state and local governments in the federal budget and is said to have amassed a personal fortune of $125 million from the fees state and local taxpayers have provided.[10]

Washington's seductive nature becomes evident when a newly elected member of the House or Senate arrives in Washington. That new, fresh-faced congressman just in from America's heartland has promised his constituents to stand tall against the alien big spenders in Washington. He is about to be given the treatment. First, a group of deferential Hill staffers show him to his suite of offices, which may well be the best he's ever occupied. The Air Force takes him on a "tour" of some of its facilities, sometimes referred to as a "junket." Lobbyists escort him to the Kennedy Center for a major musical production; foreign nations wine and dine him at embassy receptions on Massachusetts Avenue. Pretty soon, home doesn't look nearly as glamorous as Washington. With the exception of a few mavericks, it is not long before the member succumbs and becomes Washington's ambassador back to his district.

Legislators enjoy the power and perks, and they look forward to an incredibly generous pension. They don't want to give these up. They adopt a careerist mentality. They will do almost anything to get re-elected so they can stay in Washington. The best evidence of this phenomenon is what they do when they leave Congress. A good many of them stay in Washington, adding to the throng of lobbyists circling the Washington light.

As Brutus warned us in 1787 regarding our senators, they "will for the most part of the time be absent from the state they represent, and associate with such company as will possess very little of the feelings of the middling class of people. *For it is to be remembered that there is to be a federal city, and the inhabitants of it will be the great and mighty of the earth.*"[11] (Emphasis added)

> Government employees are not public servants who seek to promote the good of the people. The federal government today is much more an omnipresent "big brother" than an "Uncle Sam." Washington is not a friendly relative. Just ask anyone who has "crossed" the IRS or tried to speed up a regulatory agency.
>
> The larger the federal government has become, the more removed, faceless, independent, and unresponsive it has grown. Government employees often treat the taxpayers who foot the bill as servants, not masters.

Government employees, through civil service protection, enjoy virtual lifetime tenure, irrespective of performance. They constitute a political force of ever-increasing proportions within the federal government itself. Through their public-employee unions and associations, they heavily influence the salaries and benefits they receive, including retirement programs unmatched by those in the private sector. The very size and power of government itself is influenced by the lobbying, public relations, and media efforts of public employees fueled by taxpayer dollars.

PROPRIETARY INTERESTS

Another current political reality in Washington has to do with what can be termed "proprietary interests." Any senator or member of the House who has been in Washington for a long time—or any new member who arrives in Washington with a careerist mentality—develops a sense of "ownership" over particular programs, departments, or agencies.

Representative Claude Pepper, whose tenure in the House challenged the memory of the most ardent Washingtonphile, was a perfect example. Pepper represented the Miami, Florida, area in Congress from January 3, 1963, until May 30, 1989, dying in office. He saw himself as the official watchdog of Social Security and other "senior" citizens' programs.[12] Tip O'Neill exhibited a sense of "ownership" over the House of Representatives, as has Nancy Pelosi, who cracks the whip over any member who threatens to think for him or herself. And she has her own airplane to fly between San Francisco and Washington.[13]

Instead of approaching congressional service as a fiduciary responsibility or a trust, too many long-standing members develop a proprietary interest or ownership interest in government. That enormous difference in outlook produces an equally enormous difference in out-come—an increasing propensity to expand government and expend more money in order to nurture that which they "own."

To many members, spending is their job. That's what they do for a living. Like a surgeon who never makes an incision, a legislator who doesn't spend is an anachronism in the eyes of liberal legislators. Most don't need to spend to be re-elected. They're "safe." But they spend anyway, because spending is their only reason for existence.

The late Senator Robert Byrd (D-WV) joked repeatedly throughout his tenure about the number of buildings and programs in West Virginia named after him. West Virginia even has a Coast Guard facility thanks to Senator Byrd, despite having no coast.

The attitude of "proprietorship" is nurtured by the virtual lifetime tenure of many members of Congress. If House and Senate terms were limited, it is much more likely that "short timers" would retain a fiduciary rather than a proprietary outlook.

Government can never be made to run like a business.

By virtue of the separation of powers built into our Constitution, the "buck" does not stop in any particular place. There is no Chief Executive Officer in the same sense as in a corporation. The president cannot make spending policy and enforce it. Congress controls spending and uses that power to influence policy, both by withholding funds and by focusing the expenditure of funds on programs to which the president objects. Congress has no true "institutional" responsibility. The primary interest of the 100 senators and 435 representatives is re-election.

While a businessman has to satisfy his customers to enjoy a flow of cash, agency heads, who get their funding from Congress (their customer), need not satisfy the people to survive. As a monopoly supplier, without competition in most of the things it does, government responds as one would expect—slowly and inefficiently. That's the way it is. The only way to reduce inefficiency in government is to reduce government.

One of the crucial misconceptions about Washington is that government is a business. While it can be made more business-like, it is not a business. The president is not a Chief Executive Officer. He cannot make spending policy and enforce it. He does not control the resources of the "company." Only Congress can spend. And over the years, especially in the Budget Act of 1974, Congress actively sought to prevent the president from rescinding or sequestering spending that he thought was misguided. (Of course, President Obama is not gripped by any sense of spending restraint or discipline, so the Pelosi/Reid spendthrift Congress is fully in tune with him.)

Congress has sought to frustrate the president's constitutional veto power. It has done this by frequently sending him a huge omnibus spending bill, rather than the usual thirteen major appropriations bills, essentially daring him to veto them and shut down much of government. These grab-bag spending monstrosities more often than not include billions for pork-barrel projects of an entirely local nature.

"INSIDE-THE-BELTWAY" LINGO

Another very important aspect of the current political reality is the "inside-the-beltway" mentality. (The "beltway" is a road circling the Nation's capital through Maryland and Virginia.) One manifestation of this mentality is Washington's new use of the English language. Winston Churchill once said that England and America are the only two nations in history separated by a common language. That is now equally true between Washington and the rest of America.

Over the years, Washington has developed its own fiscal language that amounts to a foreign tongue anywhere outside the capital beltway. It uses this language when discussing spending and taxing, in order to soften the blow on the poor taxpayer. Take the innocent phrase "spending cuts." That means reductions in federal spending, right? Wrong. Not even close. The word "cut" is used differently in

Washington than it is anywhere else. In the language of government, a cut is a reduction in the projected growth rate of spending. In other words, if a given program is expected to mushroom at 10 percent a year, and if by some miracle of congressional restrain it expands only 8 percent, it has been "cut."

Such language is intended to deceive us long-suffering taxpayers back home. The program hasn't been cut. It is still growing like an untreated tumor. While the media selectively feature "those heartless spending cuts," overall federal spending has zoomed to a peacetime record percentage of the GDP.

The only reason the liberals can get away with this linguist sleight-of-hand is the federal government uses what is called a "current services" budget. That is, each year's budget is automatically increased the next year for cost-of-living increases and new entrants. Therefore, any reduction in the automatic increase is referred to as a "cut." If we were to adopt "baseline" budgeting, which uses the prior year's actual spending as the baseline, we could put a stop to the liberals' rules of the budgetary game.

One of the most frightening phrases is "tax expenditure." It is used by the politicians and bureaucrats to describe a provision of the tax code which enables you to retain part of what you earn. What it indicates is a Washington state of mind that everything you earn belongs to the government, but that by government's grace you get to keep something. That which you retain is as much an "expenditure" of taxes as government's purchase of a missile or payment of the salary of a federal judge. It is "newspeak" reminiscent of Orwell's *1984*.[14]

"Entitlements" and "automatic" are among the most repugnant words in Washington's lexicon. No longer do we provide "assistance" to those "down on their luck," we owe them sustenance; hence, they are "entitled" to be supported. And the benefits are automatically adjusted by statute for inflation or other changes so that Congress can duck the responsibility of having to vote on them. Congress has put much of the budget on automatic pilot so it can claim that increases are out of its hands.

DETACHMENT FROM CONSTITUENCIES

As the professional class in Washington grows, Congressmen acquire fiefdoms, and both parties use the federal budget to reward friends and punish enemies; basic contact with constituencies and communities break down. More and more, municipalities and other government entities at the state level have to hire a professional class of lobbyist to represent them within the halls of Congress. *Municipal governments hire lobbyists to serve as liaisons to their Congressmen.* An example is Macon, Georgia.

In a memorandum dated June 18, 2010, the lobbying firm Blank Rome reported to the Mayor and City Council of Macon, Georgia, just what it had done. The lobbyists noted that they "scheduled and organized meetings for the Mayor to brief the congressional offices" on twelve requests. They secured in excess of $2 million for special projects. The lobbyists set up meetings between city officials and federal government agencies.

It is not just Macon, Georgia. Across the country, local governments are using local tax dollars to hire lobbyists to open the doors of the very congressmen who should already be mindful of the needs of their communities, in addition to opening the doors of the professional, technocratic bureaucrats who increasingly believe they are our masters.

CHAPTER 8

GARDEN VARIETY PLUNDER

*Sometimes the law defends plunder and participates in it.... But
how is this legal plunder to be identified? Quite simply. See if the law
takes from some persons what belongs to them and gives it to the
other persons to whom it doesn't belong. See if the law benefits one
citizen at the expense of another by doing what the citizen himself
cannot do without committing a crime.*

*Then abolish that law without delay. For it is not only an evil in
itself but also a fertile source for further evils because it invites
reprisals and imitation. If such a law—which may not be an isolated
case—is not abolished immediately, it will spread, multiply and
develop into a system....*[1]

—FREDERICK BASTIAT, *THE LAW*, 1850

Some of our government's activities, like maintaining the court system or
providing the defense for the nation, are known as "public goods"—
benefits reaped equally by all taxpayers. Other programs, though
extremely expensive, are justified by officious bureaucrats as necessary
for helping the poor—or "low income," to use government-speak.

The Administration for Children and Families is the government
agency responsible for overseeing most of the federal spenders' sacred
cows—like TANF (Temporary Assistance for Needy Families, formerly
known as welfare), LIHEAP (Low Income Heating and Energy

Assistance Program, through which 8.3 million have their heat and air conditioning paid for),[2] and Head Start. ACF's annual budget of $51 billion a year is more than the Department of Homeland Security,[3] the Justice Department,[4] or the State Department.[5] Think about that number for a moment. Their budget of $51 billion,[6] the amount of money they have to spend every year, is greater than the entire Gross Domestic Product of more than half of the *countries* in the world.[7]

Yet programs for the poor represent only part of the government's redistribution scheme. Most federal spending conveys only private benefits to select groups, whether the poor, providers of favored services, makers of preferred technology, or inhabitants of a particular geographical area.

For instance, taxpayer-subsidized AMTRAK certainly benefits an easily definable class—those who ride it. Yet all taxpayers subsidize it to the tune of billions of dollars per year. As Tad DeHaven of Cato has reported, "Amtrak has lost money every year of its existence, and it has consumed almost $40 billion in federal operating and capital subsidies. During the 2000s, Amtrak averaged annual losses in excess of $1 billion. In 2010, Amtrak received $563 million in operating subsidies and $1 billion in capital and debt service grants. The American Recovery and Reinvestment Act of 2009 pumped an additional $1.3 billion in capital grants into Amtrak...

> Some people argue that other forms of transportation are subsidized, so why not passenger rail? In 2004, the Department of Transportation published a report on the cost of federal subsidies for automobiles, buses, airplanes, transit, and passenger rail per thousand passenger miles. The survey covered 1990 to 2002. In every year except one, passenger rail was the most subsidized mode of transportation. For example, in 2002 Amtrak subsidies per one thousand passenger miles were $210.31. By contrast, the subsidy for automobiles was

$1.79, which means that drivers more than supported themselves through federal fuel taxes...

As it is currently structured, passenger rail is a cost-ineffective mode of transportation. As former senator Russell Long once said, why is the government trying to get people "to leave a taxpaying organization, the bus company, and ride on a tax-eating organization, Amtrak?" Passenger rail might make economic sense on some corridors in the United States, but the only way to figure out which routes and services make sense is to let private enterprise take the lead in a deregulated marketplace...

Anthony Haswell, who in 1967 founded the National Association of Railroad Passengers and is referred to as the "father" of Amtrak, later said, "I feel personally embarrassed over what I helped to create." Joseph Vranich, a former Amtrak spokesman and rail expert, also came to recognize that it was a mistake: Amtrak is a massive failure because it's wedded to a failed paradigm. It runs trains that serve political purposes as opposed to being responsive to the marketplace. America needs passenger trains in selected areas, but it doesn't need Amtrak's antiquated route system, poor service, and unreasonable operating deficits.[8]

Taxpayers also pay farm subsidies because the government mandates it. Everyone, including other farmers and ranchers who are not subsidized, is taxed so that funds can be redistributed in the form of price supports and direct payments to a select group of people engaged in the production of wheat, corn, cotton, and a handful of other crops. And for what? To not produce or to overproduce so we must transport and store their products, artificially raising the prices we pay—so we pay twice. It encourages the government to dump our commodities abroad where they destroy local agriculture that we are at the same time trying to improve by funding Peace Corps volunteers.

Milton Friedman observed that in the 19th century, when more than half our population lived on farms, farmers would never have dreamed of farm price supports. They would have had to tax themselves to pay themselves subsidies. Now that they constitute only a tiny fraction of our population, farmers—and their representatives in Congress—can benefit mightily from the U.S. Treasury while paying only a small part of the bill.

And yet many farmers—those who are good businessmen, control their debt structure, and employ up-to-date, scientific agricultural techniques—want an end to subsidies and government interference in agriculture.[9]

When Newt Gingrich and company took charge of the House of Representatives in 1995, they vowed to end farm subsidies. In 1996 Congress passed, and President Clinton signed, the Federal Agriculture Improvement and Reform Act (FAIR), which was to phase out price supports and other federal farm programs. It didn't last. By 2002 subsidy payments were substantially increased and new crops added to the subsidy rolls. About 90 percent of subsidies still go to the "big five" crops: wheat, corn, soybeans, rice, and cotton. More than 800,000 farmers and land owners receive subsidies, but approximately 70 percent of the subsidies go to about 10 percent of the recipients, large farms and agri-businesses.

"Direct payments," which account for about $5 billion a year, are not related to current production. As Chris Edwards of Cato reported, "A substantial amount of these payments are made to owners of land that is no longer even used for farming. The *Washington Post* estimated that between 2000-2006, the United States Department of Agriculture handed out $1.3 billion in direct payments to people who don't farm. The newspaper pointed to thousands of acres of land previously used for rice-growing in Texas. The land is now used for suburban housing and other purposes, but the landowners continue to receive farm subsidies."[10] So much for helping poor family farms.

FARMING THE GOVERNMENT

As Mitzi Ayala, Past-President of American Agri Women, explained, "The government's Byzantine system of wasteful subsidies encourages some people to become farmers just so they can 'farm the government.'" Speaking from personal experience as a rice grower in Davis, California, Miss Ayala continued, "Since someone figured out a way to take advantage of the rice-subsidy, the number of rice growers in my county has grown to 72 from 50. They are not planting rice because Americans suddenly have discovered a passion for Rice-A-Roni."[11]

To understand why subsidies have created more rice farmers, consider the hypothetical example of "Farmer Brown." Farmer Brown owns a 2,000-acre parcel of rice land, slightly more than double the size of the average California rice farm. Under the rice-subsidy program, which was set up to protect small farms, his maximum payment is $50,000 year. Farmer Brown knows exactly how many acres of rice to plant to reach that limit, roughly 200. Any rice he plants beyond the 200 acres will not be profitable.

Does that mean that he takes his remaining 1,800 acres out of rice production? Not at all. Instead, he rents 200 acres each to nine others, who grow just enough rice to get their maximum $50,000 payments in government subsidies. These nine other farmers probably never grew rice before, and they certainly would not be doing so now if it weren't for the subsidies.

Opponents to abolishing farm subsidies argue that farmers would go out of business without them. They ignore the inconvenient fact that New Zealand did away with their farm subsidies in 1984, despite being significantly more dependent on farming than the U.S. As Chris Edwards of the Cato Institute explained:

The changes were initially met with fierce resistance, but New Zealand farm productivity, profitability, and output have soared since the reforms. New Zealand's farmers have cut costs, diversified their land use, sought nonfarm income, and developed nice markets such as kiwifruit.

Today, data from the Organization for Economic Cooperation and Development show that farm subsidies in New Zealand represent just 1 percent of the value of farm production, which compares to 11 percent in the United States. New Zealand's main farm organization argues that the nation's experience "thoroughly debunked the myth that the farming sector cannot prosper without government subsidies." That myth needs to be debunked in the United States as well.[12]

If ever there was justification for the redistribution game known as farm subsidies, it has long since evaporated. If the federal government had never tampered with agriculture, an orderly attrition of farmers would have taken place year by year. That's what has happened in the beef cattle industry, which is not subsidized. The less efficient producers got out of the business, and those remaining have had to adjust to changes in American's eating habits. That is the way it should be.

GLOBAL WARMING'S "CAP-AND-TRADE"

Key climate experts at the Competitive Enterprise Institute (CEI) have looked at cap-and-trade and declared that it is simply government control over energy use with massive kickbacks to favored corporations in the form of "windfall profits." Says Myron Ebell, Director of Energy Policy at CEI, "Cap-and-trade regulation, far from disciplining the energy sector, is poised to become one of the greatest wealth transfers from consumers to private corporations in the Nation's history. General Electric, Exelon, BP, Goldman Sachs and Duke Energy will make out like bandits because of provisions they have written. That's not democracy or capitalism. It's political corruption and crony capitalism."[13]

Al Gore is en route to making millions personally from his global warming "crusade." He, Barack Obama , other key Chicago political activists and, yes, Goldman Sachs, cooked up the Chicago Climate Exchange to trade the "carbon credits" which they anticipate will flow out of the "cap-and-trade" bill they've created, sponsored by Senators John Kerry (D-MA) and Joe Lieberman (I-CT). If we taxpayers allow this cap-and-trade system to be imposed, Gore and his associates will own the "turnstile" through which the carbon "permits" will pass.

All of this mischief started innocently—or so it seemed—when a federal bureaucrat sought extra funding for his agency. James Hansen, the head of Goddard Laboratory of NASA, wanted a half-billion shot in the arm. He appeared before then-Senator Al Gore's committee and explained that things were happening in the atmosphere that he didn't understand, so he needed additional funds to study "global climate change." He got the money. Interestingly, about the only people whose studies got funded by Hansen thereafter were those who agreed with the thesis that the globe was warming, that such warming was the result of man's nefarious and harmful conduct, and that we simply had to significantly reduce carbon and CO_2 emissions. Out of this have grown Kyoto, Copenhagen, and massive efforts to shut down the free-enterprise system, as we have known it, based on the mythology of man-made global warming.

DEFENSE PROGRAMS

Congress's redistribution propensities are not confined to civilian life. Senators and representatives work hard to get defense contracts for their constituents. And prime defense contractors try to "spread the wealth," seeking sub-contractors in as many districts as possible, so that their political reach and clout among members of the House and Senate are maximized. This is a type of redistribution, but the major problems with the Defense Department are far more deep-rooted and challenging. They include huge cost overruns on virtually every weapons-system procurement, massive delays with projects, and virtually catastrophic mismanagement of funds and accounting for assets.

In his recent letter to the newly-formed Commission on Fiscal Responsibility and Reform, Senator Tom Coburn (R-OK) cited both overrun costs and lack of fiscal controls in the Defense Department. In part he said, "The errors are not random: actual costs always turnout to be much higher than, sometimes even multiples of, early estimates. The reason is simple: the Pentagon doesn't know how it spends its money. In a strict financial accountability sense, it doesn't even know if the money is spent. This incomprehensible condition has been documented in hundreds of reports over three decades from both the Government Accountability Office and the Department's own Inspector General.... Amazingly, it gets worse overall; "audit trails" are not kept "in sufficient detail," which means no one can track the money; DOD's "Internal Controls," intended to track the money, are inoperative. Thus, DOD cost reports and financial statements are inaccurate, but the size, even the vector, of the errors cannot be identified because the data cannot be verified; and DOD does not observe many of the laws that govern all this.

"That final finding is perhaps the most appalling. Congress and the Pentagon annually report and hold hearings on all this and sometimes enact new laws, but nothing changes. Many of the new laws simply permit the Pentagon to ignore the previous ones."[14]

Still, Congress, not the Pentagon, deserves the main blame for cost overruns since it holds the purse strings. Rather than looking out for taxpayer interests, most members of Congress fight attempts to reduce defense spending in their districts, including spending on weapons that the Pentagon doesn't even want.

Defense contractors exploit this parochial self-interest of legislators, and they skillfully spread out research and production work across many states and districts to maximize congressional support. The $70 billion F/A-22 fighter program provides an example. The *Washington Post* noted in 2005 that the F/A-22 "is an economic engine, with 1,000 suppliers—and many jobs—in 42 states, guaranteeing solid support in Congress." In 2009, Defense Secretary Robert Gates wanted to cancel further orders of the aircraft, but hundreds of lawmakers and state governors lobbied President Obama to keep the production lines going to preserve the 95,000 related jobs.[15]

Some time ago the Air Force decided it did not need any more T-46 trainer aircraft. The contractor for the craft, Fairchild Industries, happened to manufacture the T-46 in the Long Island, New York, district of the late chairman of a powerful House defense committee. The chairman, and others in the New York delegation, insisted that more T-46's be included in the Air Force budget...and they were.[16]

REDISTRIBUTION "TRAFFIC COPS"

The main beneficiaries of the great redistribution game are the "traffic cops" in Washington who handle the money and direct its use. Think of them as brokers: bureaucracy gets an administrative fee; legislators get a political "finder's fee" (re-election commitments, campaign funds, and more); and the lobbyists—rent-seekers in chief—get the keys to the vault.

Politicians derive their power and ensure their political futures by providing special benefits to some at the expense of the general taxpayer. Congress has created a web of redistribution that is a politician's delight and a taxpayer's nightmare. Federal taxes taken from Californians are used to fill potholes on New York expressways; New Yorkers are taxed to build a waterway in Tennessee; from Tennessee, federal tax funds flow to California to purchase more "wilderness"

land to keep the environmentalists happy. If these projects are merito-
rious, let those who will benefit pay for them directly. It is ludicrous
to route our tax dollars through Washington, which, as "a system that
increasingly has Congress, in effect, buying the support of voters with
their own money is self-destructive and, frankly, ignoble,"[17] as the
Wall Street Journal astutely observed.

CHAPTER 9

ENTITLEMENT REFORM

The marvel of all history is the patience with which men and women submit to burdens unnecessarily laid upon them by their governments.[1]

—GEORGE WASHINGTON

When President Franklin Roosevelt succeeded in getting Congress to pass his Social Security scheme in 1935, he proudly proclaimed the creation of an old-age retirement system into which all Americans (and their employers) would make a contribution and from which all would receive retirement income. This was to provide a "safety net" for all Americans but was not meant to be a substitute for investments, private savings, and pensions.

However, several conceptual and investment problems with the program have now come back to haunt us. There was no "trust fund" as we understand the concept, i.e., no investment in real world, growing independent assets. The money flowed in and was paid out to the then-current beneficiaries. For many years any excess was "borrowed" by the federal government to pay for other federal programs. IOUs of the federal government were placed in the trust fund.[2] But, of course, to redeem those IOUs for the benefit of the trust fund, the beneficiaries of Social Security will have to pay higher taxes to be able to pay themselves the Social Security they are due. It was a Ponzi scheme from the beginning.

- But the nature of the Social Security scheme wasn't immediately apparent. There were initially 42 workers for every Social Security recipient, so the base of payers was very broad for each Social Security recipient.[3]
- The life expectancy was 58 for males and 62 for females. Consequently, many would die at about the time they were to receive Social Security.[4]
- The pay-in to Social Security remained only a small percentage of the worker's paycheck and only up to a small portion of his total pay.

The current realities are far different:

- There are now three workers for every retired recipient of Social Security and soon there will be just two.
- Males and females are now living much longer.
- The "contribution" is now a very significant 6-plus percent of both the worker's wages/salary and the company's payroll; and that percentage is applied to all wages up to $82,000 of the worker's pay per year.[5] If this level of contribution were invested at any reasonable compounded annual rate of return, every retiree would be very comfortable, if not downright wealthy.

- Remember, this is just a relatively small annuity. There is no corpus (or estate) to pass on to your survivors.
- And, worst of all, for young workers today the real rate of return on the Social Security "investment" will be 1 percent or less. This is an investment and retirement disaster... and entirely unfair for everyone forced to be in the Social Security program.

In a perfect world, we would not have a Social Security system. The government should no more be able to force you to invest your own money than require you to buy health insurance. Sadly, we do not live in a perfect world. There are, however, alternatives that give individuals more freedom and more control over their own destiny and money. If we cannot scrap the entire system, a solution that would be difficult politically, we should at least move toward a more market-based, individual freedom-oriented system.

ALTERNATIVE TO SOCIAL SECURITY: THE RYAN PROPOSAL

Recently, Congressman Paul Ryan (R-WI) has championed such an alternative, as have a number of other conservative congressmen and senators, from Senator Jim DeMint (R-SC) to Congressman Mike Pence (R-IN). At present, the Ryan plan is receiving active consideration among Republicans and is very much worth examining. (Although, Congressman Ryan includes his Social Security reform plan in a larger plan with a value added tax [VAT] which conservatives should shy away from.)

In his January 2010 "A Roadmap for America's Future—Version 2.0,"[6] Congressman Ryan, Ranking Member, House Committee on the Budget, proposed to allow each worker to choose a (partial) private option for investing his/her Social Security contribution. Here are the congressman's recommendations:

Personal Choice in Retirement Accounts: Beginning in 2012, the proposal allows each worker younger than 55 to shift a portion of his or her Social Security payroll tax payment into a personal retirement account, chosen from a group of investment funds approved by the government. When fully phased in, the personal accounts will average 5.1 percentage points of the current 12.4-percent Social Security payroll tax.

The personal investment component is phased in to allow a smooth transition. Initially, workers are allowed to invest 2 percent of their first $10,000 of annual payroll into personal accounts, and 1 percent of annual payroll above that up to the Social Security earnings limit. The $10,000 level will be indexed for inflation. After 10 years, the amount that workers can invest will be increased to 4 percent up to the inflation-adjusted level, and 2 percent above that. After 10 more years, these amounts will be increased to 6 percent and 3 percent. Eventually, by 2042, workers will be able to invest 8 percent up to the inflation-adjustment level, and 4 percent of payroll above that, for an account averaging 5.1 percent.

The choice of personal retirement accounts is entirely voluntary. Even those under 55 can remain in the current system if they choose. Further, those who choose to enter the personal account system also have an opportunity to leave the system, and those who initially opt out of the system of personal accounts can enter into it later on.

Property Right: Each personal account is the property of the individual, and the resources accumulated can be passed on to the individual's descendants. This contrasts with current government Social Security benefits, which are subject to reductions or other changes by Congress, and which cannot be passed on. The benefits of the personal accounts are tilted in favor of low-income individuals who do not have disposable income to invest. As a result, these individuals will be able to join the investor class for the first time. As Social Security benefits become an individual's property, the government no longer will be able to raid this money to pay for spending on other programs.

Soundness of Accounts: Those choosing the personal account option will select from a list of managed investment funds approved by the government for soundness and safety. After an account reaches a low threshold, a worker will be enrolled in a "life cycle" fund that automatically adjusts the portfolio based on age. A worker may continue with the life cycle option or choose from a list of five funds similar to the Thrift Savings Plan options. After workers accumulate more than $25,000 in their account, they can choose to invest in additional nongovernment options approved by the Personal Social Security Savings Board."[7]

Ryan's ideas on Social Security reform move us in the right direction toward greater individual freedom and control of one's own money. But let's consider an alternative from the real world.

THE CHILEAN MODEL FOR SOCIAL SECURITY REFORM

In the 1970s, Chile was experiencing disastrous results with its Social Security system. It was going broke...and the government's promises to its citizens were about to be broken.

The Chilean government turned to renowned Noble Laureate Economist Milton Friedman and his "Chicago boys" (the Economics Department at the University of Chicago) and asked for help. José Piñera, then the Minister of Labor for the Chilean government, and now a fellow with the Cato Institute, worked out a private investment pension alternative to Chile's Social Security. Chileans were given a choice between staying in the old Social Security system or moving to the new private system. Piñera describes the Chilean experience:

> The good news: there is an alternative that works. It was developed in Chile where a pay-as-you-go social security system had been started in 1925, more than a decade before it was enacted in the United States. Instead of paying a payroll tax, every Chilean worker sends his monthly contribution— between 10 percent and 20 percent of wages—to a tax-deferred pension savings account. This is the individual's private property. An individual can easily find out how much is in his or her pension savings account. Now the biggest asset of Chilean workers isn't their used car or their mortgaged home. Their biggest asset is the capital accumulated in their pension savings account. These contributions are invested in capital markets through private investment managers, yielding real positive rates of return. There are some interventions, including guidelines to exclude highly risky investments from pension savings accounts, but there aren't any compulsory investments, certainly not government securities. Chilean workers have become a nation of business owners—capitalists.
>
> In Chile, if you aren't satisfied with the way your pension savings account funds are being managed, you can switch to another investment company, known in Chile as an AFP. When you change jobs, you take your pension savings account with you. It's as portable as your bank account.
>
> Moreover, Chileans can now decide when they wish to retire. A worker figures how much he has accumulated thus far in his pension savings account and what additional percentage must be deducted from each paycheck so that when his chosen retirement date arrives, he will be able to buy an

annuity yielding 50 percent of his last wages...

What about poor people? I don't believe anybody should be barred from having a private pension account just because they're poor. That somebody might be poor at, say, age 25, doesn't mean they'll be poor at 40. With the Chilean system, everybody goes through life contributing at least 10 percent of their earnings. If by the time a man reaches 65, or a woman 60, an individual can't afford to buy an annuity yielding a minimum income, then the government supplements their accumulated capital to reach that level.

But we retained the vital link between work and reward. The more you put into your pension savings account, the more you will be able to take out. This is in dramatic contrast with Chile's government-run pension system. Workers paid up to 25 percent of their salaries into it, yet by 1980 it was broke. Like U.S. Social Security, the government-run Chilean system paid out often meager benefits which weren't related to individual effort and contributions, so there was a lot of discontent. And like U.S. Social Security, the government limited the ability of people to collect—with any pay-as-you-go government pension system, free choice about retirement age isn't allowed, because somebody else would be forced to finance your early retirement.

Moreover, politics had resulted in special privileges concerning when people could collect from their government-run pension. Factory workers couldn't collect until after age 65, white-collar workers, after 55. Bank employees could begin collecting after 25 years of work, members of Congress, after only 15 years!

Why give government such incredible power over your life? Working or not working has a lot to do with human happiness. There are some people who enjoy working well into

122

their 80s. Others want to collect pension income and go fishing at 50.

How to handle the transition from a government-run system to a private pension saving system? In Chile, we had three rules, which entailed a degree of compulsion.

First, we continued paying the elderly who had become dependent on the government-run system. We didn't touch those benefits. Second, we offered every worker the freedom to stay in the government-run system at his own risk. Or the worker could leave the system completely and begin his or her own pension savings account. Third, we required new entrants to the labor force to join the pension savings account system, because we believed it was irresponsible to go on burdening our children and grandchildren with an unfunded debt...

Initially, I encountered skepticism. Many were against the proposed new system. It meant radical change and seemed risky. Nobody else in the world had done anything like this. *Why not be the first*? I suggested. Someone has to be first. [Since then, eleven other Latin American countries have followed suit, building on the Chilean model.]

After a while, people everywhere were talking about the proposed pension savings account. They began asking when a new law would come.

While popular support was growing for it, there were formidable interest groups against it. Labor union bosses declared that pensions must not be based on individual choice. They were opposed to having pension contributions managed by private investment managers. The bosses demanded power to control where pension contributions went. The bosses made clear they would do everything they could to make my life difficult if I didn't yield to their demands.

Despite critics who warned people not to trust the private sector, the response was enormous. During the first month, 25 percent of Chilean workers—about 500,000—opted out of the government-run system. By the end of the first year, 70 percent of Chilean workers chose to open tax-deferred pension savings accounts. By the end of the second year, 90 percent had.

Individuals opting for private pension savings accounts received a recognition bond (zero coupon, indexed to inflation with 4 percent interest), which recorded their contribution to the government-run system. Upon retirement, this bond was cashed and added to their assets available to purchase an annuity.

As I mentioned earlier, after the new law took effect, people who started working for the first time made payroll contributions to their own pension savings accounts, not the government-run system. There hasn't been anybody entering the government-run system.

Yes, moving away from a pay-as-you-go system was a challenge. There was a transition gap: the amount of money we ceased to collect from workers who opted out of the system, yet had to pay current and future retirees. The transition gap was around 3 percent of our gross national product. We paid a substantial portion by reducing wasteful government spending and by using debt financing. As a consequence, we went to private pension accounts without increasing taxes, inflation, or interest rates. During the last six years, we have had government budget surpluses equal to 1 percent or 2 percent of GNP...

Going to pension savings accounts helped boost the economy, because it has raised the saving rate—now about 27 percent of GNP—and people's contributions became available for private capital markets. Since pension savings accounts got started, they have generated capital equivalent to 40 percent of Chilean GNP. During the past dozen years, annual growth has been about 7 percent, double our historic growth rate. Faster economic growth made it easier to handle the transition gap.

The real rate of return on private pension accounts has been about 12 percent. Pensions are already 50 percent to 100 percent higher than with the government-run system.

Chile has eliminated the payroll tax, which, by making it more expensive for employers to create jobs, put a damper on employment....

To be sure, Chile embraced many other free-market reforms which helped accelerate economic growth. We went to free trade, cut income taxes, privatized state-owned companies, and so on, but according to many observers, the most important reform has been the pension reform.

I believe that the way to cut the size of government is not only to reduce government programs but to abolish them. I long for the day, fast approaching, when the last person in Chile's government-run system retires and 100 percent of workers are making contributions into their own pension savings accounts.

Just imagine how this idea could energize the U.S. economy. More people would see their own efforts, not the government's, as offering the key to their future. Trillions of dollars would become available to help finance economic growth. Payroll taxes would be cut and ultimately eliminated, contributing to higher employment, higher wages, or both. Individuals would gain freedom to control their pension savings. They would almost certainly have more retirement income and greater peace of mind. It would be hard to think of a single economic reform that would do more good for everyone.[8]

Piñera makes a compelling case for immediately moving to private accounts, as Chile did, without a long-term transition. Such a transition risks congressional tinkering over time, as we observed with farm subsidy termination gradualism, which left subsidies in place to be ramped up again when times grew too tough for powerful farm interests. If the private account transition were instantaneous, a broad enough base of workers would become quickly vested with personally owned accounts that were growing rapidly so as to mitigate against any reversal of the process.

Meanwhile, back at the Obama government control "ranch," something worse than the current Social Security bankruptcy is brewing. As the annual deficit soars, and the accumulated public debt heads in the direction of a serious, if not fatal, 90 percent of GDP, Obama-focused congressional liberals are eying the trillions of dollars in cash, stocks and other investments held by pension funds in the form of privately-owned 401k accounts. Obama liberals are considering trying to take these accounts in exchange for a promise of a specific rate of return above inflation—and then spend the resources on current budget needs—leaving nothing but current taxes (and borrowings) with which to honor the obligation—not unlike current Social Security.[9] This is the kind of treachery we must guard against as we seek responsible reform of Social Security, which must occur immediately. Let's accelerate the conversion to a private pension plan by immediately means-testing Social Security. If we do it in the name of our children and grandchildren, most wealthy seniors will applaud.

ObamaCare

As if our existing runaway entitlements weren't enough, Obama and the Democrats in Congress created a new one. ObamaCare was passed against the will of the vast majority of Americans. Since then, the lies and misrepresentations used to pull off the biggest public policy heist in the Nation's history have been emerging with shocking regularity. Among the most egregious are:

Loss of Private Insurance Plans. Despite President Obama's incessant pledge that everyone would be able to keep their current insurance plan if they liked it, hidden in the 2400-page legislative monstrosity is the fine print that will induce numerous large employers to dump their employee healthcare coverage altogether. John C. Goodman, President of the National Center for Policy Analysis and a well-respected expert on healthcare issues, has indicated that many large employers are calculating that they would be well ahead financially by dropping health insurance for their employees, paying a fine of $2,000 per employee and leaving their employees with the option of buying health insurance in the newly-established exchange subsidized by the taxpayers.[10]

Small Business ObamaCare "Penalty" Will Kill Jobs, Up Costs. Employers will be socked with a $3,000 per-year per-employee penalty for any low-income employees for whom health insurance premiums exceed an arbitrary threshold. Profits will plummet, jobs will be lost, and many employers will reduce hours worked per employee to less than 30 so they can avoid providing healthcare coverage without ObamaCare penalties. And the phase-out of the small business tax credit for employers with more than 10 employees and average annual wages above $25,000 will be another sure job-killer.[11]

Individual Mandate (to purchase healthcare insurance) Challenged as Unconstitutional. Twenty-plus states are now challenging the ObamaCare requirement that all United States citizens purchase healthcare insurance.[12] Never before in the history of our Nation has the federal government ever sought to require that—essentially as a condition of citizenship—one purchase a particular good or service. After months of claiming the individual mandate is not a tax, the Obama Administration's defense of the mandate in federal court is that this is just another tax. It is, in fact, another example of the federal government using the tax code to enact social policy.

"Hidden" ObamaCare Costs Continue. CBO estimates that ObamaCare will exceed $1 trillion over 10 years, and that's without adjusting for Medicare "cuts" that won't happen, and subsidizing the uninsured and those whose private-employer healthcare plans will be discarded by employers in favor of low cost "penalties."[13] Government cost estimates are as often as not, way off the mark. Economist Larry Hunter, President of the Social Security Institute, has warned, "One thing we learned from the Medicare experience is that the original estimates of radical new government programs are, vastly understated because of government's inability to control program costs and the impossibility of imposing price controls (by whatever name) on an entire economy-wide industry. But price controls and spending caps it will be, just as it would have been with HillaryCare, followed by healthcare rationing, just as it has been with Medicare. Although these bureaucratic machinations will harm people, they won't appreciably hold down costs. At its inception in 1966, Medicare cost $3 billion a year. At that time, the Ways and Means Committee of the U.S. House of Representatives projected 'conservatively' that the program would cost approximately $12 billion a year by 1990. In 1990, the cost of Medicare was actually $107 billion—nine times greater than the Ways and Means estimate.[14]

There is only one responsible path which America should follow in response to ObamaCare: We must de-fund ObamaCare and totally start over—on our terms. This can happen only in 2011, after the midterm elections.

THE FALSE PREMISES OF CURRENT HEALTHCARE

We must start by challenging every one of the Obama/Leftist false premises:

- That healthcare is a government, societal, or collective issue rather than a private relationship between doctor and patient.
- That delivery of healthcare should be tied to employment. When people frequently change jobs, as they do today, employment is no longer a relevant connection. But the giant private healthcare insurance companies find perpetuation of this myth in their profit interest.
- That healthcare should be the province of third-party payers—government or private—thereby assuring that there will be no cost-conscious consumers of health services who will ever be able to discipline costs, control prices, and increase quality as they do in every other aspect of the marketplace that is truly competitive.
- That an unconstitutional mandate on individuals to buy insurance is necessary to "force" healthy young people into the "pool" to spread the cost of coverage for high-risk people and satisfy the political demands of the healthcare insurance industry.
- That self-insurance—or a conscious decision to pay out-of-pocket for medical services—is not an acceptable alternative in a free society.

HISTORY OF HEALTHCARE INSURANCE

A little history is in order for us to find a proper solution to the healthcare dilemma. Before World War II, families had family doctors—and paid them directly, thereby controlling pricing by creating competition between doctors and hospitals. World War II changed all that.

Employers, hamstrung by wage and price controls, found they could compete for good workers (those who had not already gone off to war as soldiers and sailors) only by creating attractive non-wage benefits.

The benefit they seized on was healthcare, which they provided via employer-paid healthcare insurance. This was the first time "insurance" became part of healthcare. And it was not simply insurance for major or catastrophic problems—as in car insurance—but it was payment for the "tires, batteries, and lube jobs" of healthcare, as well.

Since that time, Americans have never been able to determine, nor compete and negotiate with respect to, real healthcare costs. Our only debate has been over healthcare insurance premiums, not direct healthcare costs.

ELIMINATE THIRD-PARTY PAYERS

We must abandon altogether healthcare reform that involves third-party payers—government or private—and create cost-conscious and aware consumers of medical services. Otherwise, we will never bring healthcare costs under control and get Washington out of the healthcare business.

We treat welfare recipients as more intelligent than Medicare recipients. We give someone on welfare cash to spend on food, shelter, clothes, and other necessities, counting on them to negotiate the best prices and terms possible. But for that same welfare recipient, as well as Medicare recipients and millions of workers who receive health insurance through their employers, medical services are paid for by third parties—public and private—leaving the beneficiaries ignorant and clueless as to comparative costs and quality. As a result, their demands on the system are virtually limitless because the medical services are perceived as essentially free, putting relentless upward pressure on healthcare costs.

There is only one way to contain healthcare costs: create knowledgeable, cost-conscious consumers who have a personal incentive to "shop" for healthcare—as they do for other products and services—and who will force prices down through competition.

To be able to achieve this goal, we must eliminate the costly middle-man, i.e., third-party payers (whether government or private) and let people return to controlling their own healthcare, as they do their jobs, finances, housing, and most everything else.

The debate over ObamaCare never extended to the creation of cost-conscious consumers because individual Americans were never at the bargaining table. Represented were the "public option" single-payer socialists and the third-party payer "private" insurance companies seeking to perpetuate their employer-driven healthcare monopoly.

Government—as well as private—healthcare providers all started from the status quo: third-party employer or government-provided conventional health insurance policies that pick up the tab for day-to-day medical services. This approach has kept all Americans totally ignorant of medical costs and has prevented them from becoming cost-conscious consumers who will discipline, control, and reduce health-care costs. Private healthcare insurance providers threw in with government medicine enthusiasts because their profit margins depended on perpetuating and expanding this anti-consumer, waste-ful, explosive cost-growth industry. Many conservative healthcare policy experts and market enthusiasts kept quiet about all this during the heat of the negotiations. They did so because of a terrible habit on the right: a refusal to criticize business. Just because an entity is a business does not make it good. Healthcare companies, like many other major companies, have been perfectly happy to game Washington for their bottom line at the expense of consumers. Conservative healthcare policy experts must not keep quiet any longer.

HEALTH INSURANCE FOR "CATASTROPHIC EVENTS"

Medical "insurance" should only provide for high-deductible cata-strophic coverage, like auto insurance. We don't buy car insurance to cover tires, batteries, and lube jobs, which are the ankle sprains, influenza, and headaches of the healthcare business. We pay auto-maintenance expenses out-of-pocket and watch every penny. We should do the same with day-to-day medical "repairs and mainte-nance" so we can keep medical insurance rates low and be prepared for the day we have a major "wreck" (hospitalization, cancer, etc.) and really need the insurance company to pick up the tab.

All of this can be done through tax-free medical savings accounts which the individual and/or employer can pay into and which have worked very well where they have been encouraged and allowed to work. In the case of welfare recipients, or others who need financial assistance, the payment into the account can be made by the gov-ernment (as is done under Governor Mitch Daniels' plan in the State of Indiana). But the beneficiary remains a cost-conscious consumer of medical services, motivated by the opportunity to keep—tax-free—at the end of the year anything left in the account. All this is backed up by a low-premium, high-deductible catastrophic health-insurance policy.

Pharmaceutical and large health-insurance companies and their associations prostituted themselves when they hired Obama syco-phants and big-government-control enthusiasts to represent them in ObamaCare negotiations. You owe them nothing. Show them the door—but open it to the grass roots, tea partiers, and small businesses that are the life-blood of our Nation, its future, and a reconstituted Republican Party. And give them an independent and truly private healthcare system worthy of our great Nation.

MEDICARE REFORMS—NOW

There is absolutely no reason why current, as well as soon-to-be recip-ients of Medicare, should not be paying their own medical bills, if they can afford to. We should means-test Medicare and, at a minimum, require that the day-to-day medical bills be borne by the individual until the deductible on a catastrophic healthcare insurance policy is reached. This will have an immediate effect of bringing down health-care costs as senior consumers "shop" for and become knowledgeable of real healthcare costs. After all, since the Medicare "trust fund" is mythology, it is not right, nor fair, that we dump onto our children and grandchildren our healthcare costs if we can afford to pay them our-selves. And certainly those seniors who can and do pay for their own normal living expenses, take cruises and other vacations, pay their lawyers, tax preparers, landscapers and other professionals, buy cars and pay for repairs, should be paying their every-day doctor visits and other medical expenses.

Those seniors unable to pay any of their medical bills can never-theless become equally cost-conscious, healthcare consumers if Medicare were to fund health savings accounts for them. They would be incentivized to purchase healthcare wisely and sparingly if they received all or a portion of the funds remaining in the account at the end of a year.

These proposals and solutions for healthcare reforms run 180 degrees counter to Obama's liberal mentality because they spring from motivations of individual freedom rather than the collectivist, central-ized-control, nationalized-healthcare mentality. But we still have time to interdict ObamaCare if we will act quickly and decisively.

MEDICAID—USE THE WELFARE REFORM MODEL AND MEDICAL SAVINGS ACCOUNTS

The 1996 Welfare Reform Act was a huge success. Workfare became the hallmark of the reform with finite federal block-grant funding to the states with few strings attached. Incentives to expand welfare were eliminated. It resulted in significantly reduced caseloads.

The same model should be used for delivery of healthcare to the poor, with the addition of the health savings account controlled by the beneficiary. As with the Medicare reform recommendation, allow the recipient to benefit from controlling costs and outlays. Cost-conscious consumers are found at all income levels.

CHAPTER 10
DOWNSIZE GOVERNMENT

It is the responsibility of the patriot to protect his country from its government.[1]

—THOMAS PAINE

Many conservatives, disheartened by years of federal bloat under Republicans and Democrats, think it will be impossible to cut the government down to size. But we know government growth can be reversed, tax rates lowered, and debt reduced—because other nations have done it.

Over the last sixteen years, twenty-five nations have moved from progressive personal income tax structures to flat rate taxes, which have enduring benefits. They are simple and fair, promote economic growth and tax competition, and rise and fall with inflation. Far from seeing revenues drop, as opponents forecast, many of these nations have seen tax revenues actually increase because fewer people dodged the tax collector and their underground economies contracted. Compliance costs for the individual taxpayers are significantly reduced, as well.

In 1993, only one country in the world—Hong Kong—had a flat income tax. Sixteen years later, there are twenty-five, thanks to the work of tax policy advisors like Björn Tarras-Wahlberg of World Taxpayers Association and free-market economists who have relentlessly challenged their governments to collect revenue in ways that will prosper their nations, not bankrupt them. Having seen success in reforming and lowering their tax burdens, many hope to zero out their flat income taxes soon and go to consumption-based tax systems to be able to shut down their invasive tax collectors.

FLAT PROPORTIONAL INCOME TAXES[2]
From 1 to 25 countries in 16 years

Kyrgystan (since 2006)	10%	Ukraine (2004)	15%
Kazakhstan (2007)	10%	Iraq (2004)	15%
Macedonia (2007)	10%	Montenegro (2007)	15%
Mongolia (2007)	10%	Mauritius (2007)	15%
Albania (2008)	10%	Czech Republic (2008)	15%
Bulgaria (2008)	10%	Romania (2005)	16%
Nepal (2008)	10%	Slovakia (2004)	19%
Serbia (2008)	10%	Estonia (1994)	19%
Georgia (2005)	12%	Jersey and Guernsey (1940)	20%
Macau	12%	Lithuania (1994)	24%
Balarus (2009)	12%	Jamaica (1984)	25%
Russia (2001)	13%	Trinidad & Tobago	25%
Hong Kong (1947)	15%		

The United States is not on this list. It continues its job-and-consumer-killing corporate tax rate of 35 percent, second-highest in the world. When you add state corporate tax rates to the federal rate, many total over 40 percent. Is it any wonder the United States is increasingly non-competitive?

Had the United States been smart enough to eliminate its corporate income tax, or reduce it dramatically to remain competitive, intellectual property migration, an increasing phenomenon, might never have occurred.

SLASH DEBT

The United States is not the first nation to confront massive deficits, nor will it be the last. Some nations have managed to curtail spending and choke off the deficit habit with dramatic results.

DEBT REDUCTION IN ADVANCED ECONOMIES (PERCENTAGE OF GDP)[3]

COUNTRY AND PERIOD	STARTING DEBT RATIO	ENDING DEBT RATIO	PERCENT REDUCTION
Ireland (1987-2002)	109	32	77
Denmark (1991-2008)	80	22	58
Belgium (1993-2007)	137	84	53
New Zealand (1986-2001)	72	30	42
Canada (1996-2008)	102	63	39
Sweden (1996-2008)	73	38	35
Iceland (1995-2005)	59	25	34
Netherlands (1993-2007)	79	46	33
Spain (1996-2007)	67	36	31
Norway (1979-1984)	57	35	21
Average	84	41	42

How did these nations do it?

In 1994, Canada was put on a "credit watch" when its combined federal and provincial debt exceeded 100 percent of GDP. To lower its debt ratio, Canada froze the pay of its public employees, eliminated 15 percent of the federal workforce and reduced "corporate welfare" (subsidies to business and agriculture).[4]

New Zealand presents an admirable case of reform. In the 1980s, its annual deficits exceeded six percent of GDP. It had virtually zero economic growth. The reforms it adopted included removing wage and price controls, cutting public employee numbers, and slashing government spending dramatically (by more than seven percent of GDP) with the aid of privatization.[5]

As former New Zealand government minister Maurice McTigue recalled, "When we started this process (cutting government) with the Department of Transportation, it had 56,000 employees. When we finished, it had 53. When we started with the forest service, it had 17,000 employees. When we finished it had 17. When we applied it to the Ministry of Works, it had 28,000 employees. I used to be Minister of Works and ended up being the only employee.... We achieved an overall reduction of 66 percent in the size of government, measured by the number of employees."[6]

Ireland pursued reform through major tax rate and public employee reductions.

Slovakia, a significant and recent success story, constrained government spending from 65 percent to 43 percent of GDP in seven years and adopted a 19 percent flat tax rate.[7]

Sweden has been the worldwide poster-child for "democratic" socialism. But this liberal home of the Nobel Prizes has been changing its ways. It reduced healthcare subsidies, cut its personal income tax in half, repealed its "death tax" five years ago, and has experienced a resurgence in economic growth. Many wealthy people who left Sweden because of its burdensome death tax have subsequently returned.[8]

If these nations can downsize and avoid fiscal doomsday, clearly, with commitment and the right leadership, we, too, can bring down the national debt. It will require total commitment among independent, freedom-loving Americans. They must be prepared to challenge those who live off government—and like it—mainly the public employees, their unions, and the hordes of lobbyists and other "rent-seeking" special interests that congregate in Washington and its belt-way world. Those nations which have reversed course all streamlined their government workforce and its excessive costs. "Entitlement" recipients will have to be prepared for change and participation in the reform process, as well.

GOVERNMENT'S DIRTY LITTLE SECRET: THEY ALREADY KNOW HOW TO CUT WASTE

Former House Majority Leader Dick Armey brilliantly came up with a way to streamline military functions, which include unpopular base closures, with the "Defense Base Realignment and Closure Commission" (BRAC). BRAC has shown that the creation of an outside commission of independent, experienced business appointees who make recommendations is the best way to make cuts in government. Congress couldn't do it itself because each Member defers to his colleagues defending the bases in their districts when considering individual base closures. But a report that was developed by an independent commission, on objective evidence, was a different animal. Base closures as part of a larger package that would inevitably go into effect unless Congress, on a single up-or-down vote, rejected it, made reducing government less painful by removing the personal touch—along with corresponding accountability come election-time. After BRAC's implementation, we began to close military bases that we could never before terminate. The end result was not only great for American taxpayers, but some of the base facilities have been redeveloped by entrepreneurial-minded local governments and have become significant local financial benefits for the various communities.

Since 1988, there have been four successive bipartisan Defense Base Closure and Realignment Commissions (BRAC) that recommended the closure of 125 major military facilities, 225 minor military bases and installations, and the realignment in operations and functions of 145 others. By another account, the four BRAC rounds achieved 97 base closings and 55 major realignments. This resulted in net savings to taxpayers of over $16 billion through 2001 and over $6 billion in additional savings annually.[9]

The natural question now must be, how can BRAC be emulated in cutting and streamlining extra-military government functions?

The National Tax Limitation Committee has worked with Representative Todd Tiahart (R-KS) to develop a "bureaucracy closure commission" concept modeled after Dick Armey's BRAC. Currently, it is HR 1802: "Commission on the Accountability and Review of Federal Agencies Act" (CARFA). If average citizens began putting pressure on their elected representatives to refine this concept and design multiple commissions, they would prevail. Ineffective programs would be systematically terminated, while others with potential would be consolidated or devolved to the states where they belong, all the while reigniting deTouqueville's spirit of private associations and community responses. If Republicans succeed in controlling at least one House of Congress in November 2010, they can establish informal commissions modeled on BRAC to review federal programs and follow commission recommendations in the appropriations process through de-funding.

Our elected officials should be able to make decisions to cut government programs, as well. If they follow certain criteria, it will be simple to identify which programs have ceased to provide value—if they ever did in the first place. Unfortunately, inertia favors continuation of a program if no one makes waves, because every program is on "automatic pilot." The classic problem is one of concentrated benefits vs. diffused costs. A program which is without merit is, nevertheless, of value to those who are benefitting from it. Since that one program costs each of us very little, we have minimum motivation to spend enormous amounts of time, energy and resources to end it. Result: funding continues.

But now we have more visibility and transparency tools available: the OMB evaluates every program once every five years; oversight committees hold hearings; GAO performs audits; outside organizations also conduct periodic reviews. The bottom line is we now have more performance data. It is only a matter of collecting and acting on it. For example, OMB's website provides information on programs that include:

- Vocational education state grants—OMB has given this program what is essentially a flunking grade, calling it "ineffective."[10] This program has no business being re-funded. But it continues to be.
- Community development block grants—In "Meeting America's Economic Crisis: A 'Roadmap' to Emergency Federal Spending Reduction," delivered to Congress in January 1981 by the National Tax Limitation Committee, this program was cited as a failure. Nevertheless, it has continued to be funded in the 30 intervening years because it is a political slush fund for mayors and cities across America. OMB grades it as "ineffective."[11] President George W. Bush tried to cancel it in several of his budgets, only to see funding restored by Congress.

This has been happening nationwide for decades: "business as usual." Only if we change the *process* are we likely to change the *results*. In a perfect world, our congressional leaders would be willing to make the tough choices. Sadly, we've reached a point where congressmen would prefer to demagogue issues rather than actually fix things. Having Congress step up to the plate without independent commissions would be preferable, but that's extremely unlikely.

CHAPTER 11

THE RIGHT SIZE

My reading of history convinces me that most bad government results from too much government.[1]

—SENATOR JOHN SHARP WILLIAMS

Being in favor of limited government does not mean Republicans are anti-government. On the contrary, the Constitution was written because the United States *must* be governed, keeping in balance unity, justice, national defense, and our general welfare in pursuit of liberty. But the talking points Republicans use when discussing government gives the impression that they would prefer no government at all—which would result in anarchy.

If Republicans are going to be successful in turning our nation from the destructive course set by years of expanding government, they must have more of a plan than vaguely just "cutting government." To convince voters that they are serious about taming wasteful government, Republicans must set their sights on reducing Washington to its optimal (right) size. They can't succeed without the support of their colleagues in the House and Senate: Democrats and Independents. They will have a chance to gain such support by proving that the failure of both parties to limit government size in the last half of the 20th century has actually stunted our Nation's economic growth. Republicans know that excessive government cripples national economic growth and impoverishes the people. And they can win doubters over with cold, hard data.

Republicans must identify what is known as the optimal level of government, and then set the agenda to attain it—not with words and promises of spending self-control, but with institutional barriers to government growth and structural devices to assure systematic dismantling of excessive government programs and entities.

Research has shown that there is an objective level at which government quits serving its people and instead requires being served and perpetuated with tax dollars. As the late economist Gerald Scully, who studied the "optimal" size of government for years, discovered, "as the burden of government rises, national economic growth slows."[2] He estimated that the optimal size of government was no more than approximately 20 percent of GNP.[3]

He also proved that:

■ Beyond the optimal level of spending, government becomes a net drain on the economy. Up to that level, every dollar spent by government provides more than a dollar's worth of economic growth. Beyond the optimal level, every additional dollar in spending costs more than a dollar in economic growth. At today's spending level, the next dollar in taxation costs the Nation at least $2.75 in lost economic growth.[4]

■ In 1948, total spending by federal, state, and local governments in the United States was about 23 percent of GNP,
but it had grown to 35 percent by 2008. During that time,
the average annual compound growth rate of the economy
was 3.5 percent. If governments had not increased their
shares of GNP, the annual growth rate of GNP would have
been 5.8 percent per year. This would have resulted in $37
trillion more real GNP by 2004. The average American
family would be three times wealthier today as a result.[5]

Low income—or other—Americans would not have needed to "sacrifice" government largesse to achieve this result. At 23 percent of GNP
spending level, with comparable tax rates, government at all levels
would have collected over $60 trillion more in taxes, enough to have
funded all spending programs without public debt.

Going forward, if spending were reduced to 20 percent of GNP and
tax rates systematically reduced to maximize growth, by 2030 real
GNP would be double what we anticipate under current spending and
taxing plans.

Total government spending as late as the 1920s represented only 10
percent of the Nation's income: 7 percent for state and local governments, and about 3 percent for Washington. Allocation of spending
authority at different levels of government in today's world has
changed. Of the total, probably two-thirds would be national, with
one-third being state and local. But as Milton Friedman was fond of
saying, if 10 percent was the right church tithe, why should government be entitled to a greater share?

Other economists have urged even lower total government shares.
Economist and Cato scholar Dan Mitchell performed a worldwide survey of studies on "The Impact of Government Spending on Economic
Growth" in 2005. Consistently, he found that as a nation's government increases in size, its rate of economic growth is substantially

reduced. He recommended reducing government's size to 10 percent of GDP to maximize economic output.[6]

Economists James Gwartney, Randall Holcombe, and Robert Lawson determined that *there is "a strong and persistent negative relationship between government expenditures and growth of GDP...* [but] where nations reduced their government expenditures by an appreciable amount, this reduction in size of government was correlated with an increase in the growth rate of real GDP.

They concluded, "[T]here is no evidence that any country in the data sets examined in this paper had a level of government expenditures insufficient to maximize growth. Some nations had government expenditures between 15 and 20 percent of GDP and ... those countries had higher rates of growth than nations with government expenditures in the range of 20 to 25 percent of GDP. There is no evidence that any of the nations examined here had governments so small that they inhibited growth.... current government expenditures in the United States and other industrial nations indicate that [government spending on core functions] can be provided with less than 15 percent of GDP."

"It is clear that the core functions of government can be provided with less than 15 percent of GDP. Taken together, *these two findings indicate that the growth-maximizing level of government expenditures is no more than 15 percent of GDP.*"[7] (Emphasis added.)

The authors' reasons for declaring that smaller government is better for a nation's economic growth is that as government grows:

- Higher taxes and/or additional borrowing put an excess burden on the economy;
- Productivity declines;
- The political process inhibits entrepreneurship which is the discovery process vital to wealth creation;
- Government growth leads to redistribution of income and to increased regulation which encourages "rent-seeking,"

i.e., wealth transfer via lobbying and political special interest, instead of wealth creation.

Most notably, Gwartney, Holcombe, and Lawson concluded that:

■ Nations with the smallest increase in government outperformed those with the largest increases.
■ Three nations—Ireland, New Zealand, and the United Kingdom—actually shrunk the size of their governments at some point. Their economic growth rates during government shrinkage vs. government expansion are totally consistent with the authors' size-of-government analysis.
■ Government spending as a percent of GDP can drastically impact the economy. When you consider the compounding effect of such contrasting growth rates over, say, a 10-year period (66 percent national economic growth vs. less than 20 percent cumulative growth), its impact becomes even more disastrous.

The data is clear and compelling. Republicans, frequently attacked as supporting "tax cuts for the rich" or cutting government to "hurt the poor or [insert favorite class of victim here]" can stand behind reliable data. But they now have something Democrats have always had—stories.

Democrats are brilliant at putting a human face on economic stories. In passing ObamaCare, the Democrats routinely trotted out people who had been denied coverage by evil, awful insurance companies. Republicans never responded as they should have—by trotting out Canadians who waited a year for gall bladder surgery or the families of deceased victims of socialized medicine.

Here, Republicans can show national success stories—countries that increased their economic growth as they decreased government.

People presently understand that the growth of government is going to leave an insurmountable debt for generations to come. Showing that other countries were able to grow their way out of calamity by shrinking government, *while still meeting basic needs,* presents a compelling alternative to the Democratic dream of an omnipotent government running our lives and spending our money.

CHAPTER 12

"THE CHAINS OF THE CONSTITUTION"

Free government is founded in jealousy, and not in confidence. It is jealousy and not confidence which prescribes limited constitutions, to bind down those whom we are obliged to trust with power.... Our Constitution has accordingly fixed the limits to which, and no further, our confidence may go.... In questions of power, then, let no more be heard of confidence in man, but bind him down from mischief by the chains of the Constitution.[1]

—THOMAS JEFFERSON

When the Founding Fathers met in Philadelphia in 1787 to shape the United States Constitution, they determined that one of the fundamental flaws of the Articles of Confederation was that it required a unanimous vote to amend the Articles. Recognizing that the people would want to change the Constitution from time to time, consensus was reached that the amendment process should be difficult but not impossible.

The debate at Philadelphia narrowed to the question: who is to have the power to recommend and approve amendments, Congress or the states? On May 29, 1787, Edmund Randolph, Governor of

Virginia, offered the Virginia proposal which excluded the "national legislature" entirely from the amendment process, leaving that authority to the states. George Mason explained, *"It would be improper to require the consent of the national legislature, because they may abuse their power, and refuse their consent on that very account."*[2]

When the Committee of Detail reported to the convention on August 6, its draft read: "On application of the legislatures of two-thirds of the states in the Union, for an amendment of this Constitution, the legislature of the United States shall call a convention for that purpose."[3] This provision contemplated single amendments, the states alone triggered the process, the national legislature played no role except as an agent to convene the convention, and the convention method was selected as the means of not only developing the amendment but also of actually making it (ratifying it) a legally binding part of the Constitution.

On September 10, the convention debated the amendment provision. The Founders vacillated between a limited role for Congress (the Virginia plan) and a limited role for the states with no convention (the federalists' proposal). Finally, on September 15, George Mason repeated his concern that without a convention provision, Congress might never propose "amendments of the proper kind"—those that might be inimical to its power.[4] Amendment-proposing authority was affirmed for Congress, and for the states through the convention process. The separate step of ratification became the sole province of the states, requiring approval by three-fourths of the states, irrespective of whether amendments were proposed by Congress or a state-convened convention.

It is clear that the Founders, in devising the convention process for state-initiated amendments, considered it an important safeguard against, and a limit upon, an overbearing central government. They viewed the states as co-equal with Congress in proposing amendments. The convention process was not "a last resort."

ARTICLE V POWER DISCIPLINES CONGRESS

Although we've never had an Article V convention, the very fact that the procedure exists tends to keep Congress more honest and responsive. For example, early in the last century—after years of resistance by the Senate to the direct election of Senators—states began to adopt resolutions calling on Congress to pass such an amendment or to convene a constitutional convention for the purpose of framing such an amendment. When the number of state resolutions was just one shy of the required two-thirds, the Senate finally capitulated, approved an amendment, and sent it to the states for ratification. The Senators recognized that unless they designed the amendment themselves, a convention might decide not to allow them to complete their terms but, rather, require each of them to stand for election immediately.

The first Article V state resolution for an amendment to balance the budget was passed in 1975. State Senator Jim Clark in Maryland and State Representative David Halbrook in Mississippi started the drive with resolutions in their respective states.[5]

In 1979, the balanced budget amendment had garnered 29 state resolutions (34 are needed).[6] In 1979, Governor Jerry Brown of California publicly announced his support for the Article V resolution process and led an unsuccessful effort to persuade the liberal Ways and Means Committee of the California Assembly to approve the resolution. Because Jerry Brown had thrown his hat in the ring for the Democratic presidential nomination, the resolution-gathering process became embroiled in presidential politics. Carter's White House formed a task force to oppose the resolution effort. Well-coordinated opposition began to emerge.

LIBERAL "FRONT GROUP" OPPOSES STATE RESOLUTIONS

The power and importance of the state resolution process for the balanced budget amendment became as clear to the enemies of federal fiscal discipline as it was to those seeking to pass an amendment. In 1983, the AFL-CIO, and other foes of the amendment, formed a committee that they disingenuously called "Citizens to Protect the Constitution." Among those joining the AFL-CIO in their enterprise were (partial list):

American Association of University Professors
American Association of University Women
American Civil Liberties Union
American Federation of Teachers
Americans for Democratic Action
American Jewish Congress
Americans for Indian Opportunity
Americans for Religious Liberty
American Federation of State, County and Municipal Employees
B'nai B'rith International
Center for Community Change
Communication Workers of America
Consumer Federation of America
General Board of Church and Society, United Methodist Church
International Association of Machinists and Aerospace Workers
International Ladies Garment Workers
Leadership Conference on Civil Rights
National Association for the Advancement of Colored People
National Association of Letter Carriers
National Bar Association
National Education Association
National Farmers Union
National Legal Aid & Defender Association
National Organization for Women

National Urban League
National Women's Political Caucus
People for the American Way
Service Employees International Union
United Auto Workers
United Mine Workers
United Steel Workers of America.

(While the list appears to be overpopulated with labor unions, this is an anomaly. Private-sector union *members* support a balanced amendment as vigorously as do non-union workers. It is labor *leaders*, especially those in charge of unions comprised of government workers, who oppose constitutional constraints on government purse strings.)

These organizations found that "stonewalling" state constitutional convention resolutions by challenging the *substance* of the tax limitation and balanced budget amendment was not working. Nationwide, Americans overwhelmingly supported such an amendment. Consequently, opponents shifted their strategy and began generating fears of the constitutional convention *process*. They incited fears of a convention running amok—a so-called "runaway" convention—repealing the Bill of Rights and dismantling the constitutional framework.

You can imagine the frustration of those seeking Article V state resolutions when, during a legislative hearing in Michigan in 1984, representatives of the ACLU, public-employee unions, welfare-rights groups, etc., talked about our beautiful, pristine Constitution, claiming that we dare not risk changing one word or one concept in this precious document, and that a citizen convention was an unacceptable risk. These are the very same individuals and groups who, for more than half a century, have done everything possible to rewrite the Constitution, through court decisions and congressional action, in order to concentrate power in Washington and subvert the power of states, local governments, private organizations, and individuals. Having been successful in dismantling the restraints against federal intervention in state-local-private matters through redefinition of the Commerce Clause, the General Welfare Clause and so forth, these selfsame guardians of the public weal claim we cannot risk any changes in the sacred document, especially at the hands of *the people.*

Such unabashed duplicity on the part of liberals was not entirely unexpected. What was not anticipated was that some conservatives, even some experienced in the political process, would become handmaidens of the liberals trying to block the state resolution process. These included the Liberty Lobby, an overtly anti-Semitic group, the John Birch Society, Eagle Forum, and a handful of others who found themselves in league with the liberal organization listed above.

Opponents of the Article V convention process asserted the same shopworn claims and falsehoods from state to state, counting on the sheer volume of objections to scare unwitting citizens who were being exposed to the idea of Constitutional amendment for the first time. In turn, concerned constituents harassed and sought to intimidate legislators with cajolery and threats. It was political mob psychology at its worst. Sadly for the state of our budget, the effort failed and lawmakers have continued to run up our deficit, for the most part.

STATE POWER TO DISCIPLINE WASHINGTON

Though the convention to introduce a balanced budget amendment failed, the ability of states to use their Article V powers remains important as a means to rein in Congress (which will not propose certain necessary reforms of and limitations upon federal excesses) and the federal court system.[7]

The Supreme Court has rendered decisions that constitute amendments to the U.S. Constitution, such as the 1962 decision on school prayer that essentially amended the Constitution to read, "No prayer shall be offered in a public school," and the 1973 decision on abortion that, as an amendment, would have read: "Abortion shall be the right of every pregnant woman." In so doing, the Court has exercised both the proposing and ratifying powers without regard to the requirements of Article V.

We must not ignore the people's convention-calling authority. Doing so would not only forfeit the right of the people, through their states, to *initiate* amendments restraining the federal government, but would also relinquish the power to revoke "amendments" imposed on us by court decisions (wherein the people's right to "ratification" is non-existent). It is no wonder liberals have clamored to preside over the funeral of Article V's state resolution power. That power is the ultimate sword of Damocles over the Left's agenda.

The current uprising in the states over ObamaCare's "individual mandate," and state threats to exempt themselves from the provisions of federal unfunded mandates, constitute a perfect vehicle for the reassertion of state sovereignty. Use of Article V by state legislatures to propose an Amendment to remedy *one* of these problems would put an end to "runaway" convention fear-mongering. Then this power would be readily and continuously available to the states to discipline Washington. It is past time that we got started.

THE PENCE–HENSARLING–CAMPBELL FEDERAL SPENDING LIMIT AMENDMENT: ON THE RIGHT TRACK

Over twenty years after the balanced budget amendment convention failed to reach critical mass, a new federal spending limit amendment has been introduced in Congress by some of its most fiscally responsible members. Mike Pence (R-IN) is the Chairman of the House Republican Conference, responsible for charting strategy for House Republicans. Jeb Hensarling (R-TX) is past Chairman of the House Republican Study Committee (the conservative Republican alliance), and John Campbell (R-CA) serves on several key fiscal committees. All are devoted fiscal watchdogs and taxpayer champions.

Their spending limit amendment (SLA) is simple, straightforward, and on target. It limits federal spending to the right variable: Gross Domestic Product (GDP). Introducing their amendment with a recitation of the current realities of federal spending excesses, they have declared the benefits of the Amendment:

> The Spending Limit Amendment (SLA) to the Constitution of the United States would ensure that federal spending cannot grow faster than a family's ability to pay for it. The Amendment would limit spending to one-fifth of the economy—the historical average for spending since World War II. The limit could only be waived if a declaration of war was in effect or by a two-thirds vote of Congress.[8]

The SLA does not promise a particular spending plan of which programs to restrain and by how much, but rather a constitutional constraint on lawmakers present and future. As columnist George Will has said, "The Constitution stipulates destinations. It does not draw detailed maps."

But unless there is first a national consensus of the optimal size of government and its limits, it is clear that lawmakers will not be prepared to address our spending and debt crisis without asking taxpayers to pay more.

The decision to amend the Constitution can never be made lightly. However, the Founders knew that occasionally sands shift and foundations need shoring up, which is why they provided a rigorous amendment process to be used with great deference. Thomas Jefferson himself expressed a desire to amend the Constitution to limit the size of government when he stated, "*I would be willing to depend on that alone for the reduction of the administration of our government.*" Such an amendment's time has come.[9]

CHAPTER 13

THE WAY FORWARD

The people will save their government, if the government itself, will do its part, only indifferently well.[1]

—ABRAHAM LINCOLN

The New Deal and Great Society put America on a collision course with economic and regulatory disaster. Majority-rule Republicans and the Bush Administration paved the way for Obama, Reid, and Pelosi to accelerate the derailment. We can't undo the political and financial damage overnight, but we must start the healing process as soon as possible (hopefully with control of the House of Representatives in 2011 by dedicated, fiscally conservative Republicans). Republicans must set a clear course of rehabilitation and, most of all, stay on that course with absolute commitment and determination year after year for at least a decade. We know what must be done to restore America to greatness: We must fight back with every means at our disposal to bring down the size and invasiveness of government at all levels, maximize our national economic growth rate, encourage private job, business, and wealth creation, and revitalize the freedom of individuals and families to run their own lives and private relationships. This is what the tea party movement is all about and has been the mission of all of us fighting government growth for the last half-century or more.

If we are able to launch America on a glide-path to lower spending and deficits as a share of GDP, we will induce an increasing level of national economic growth that can save our Nation from fiscal disaster. It will only succeed by enlisting the aid of every thoughtful American who knows Washington is vastly over-extended and is hell-bent on rent-seeking (redistributing wealth based on political power, not performance, productivity, or wealth creation). They must be guardians of the process, and committed to the means and the outcome, carefully monitoring progress year after year.

A CHECKLIST FOR RECOVERY

Here are some of the common-sense steps we ought to take to put governments at all levels on the road to fiscal recovery:

- A statutory spending limit: We have to get consensus that total government spending should not grow—year-over-year—by more than inflation and population changes. Congressman Lamar Smith (R-TX) has picked up on this concept in HR5323, Lamar's SAFE Act.[2] If Congress failed to get spending under control and limited to this number, the President would be required to do so. The key point here is that citizens would have a specific "do-not-exceed" spending number in mind and, therefore, being a part of the process, can be part of the enforcement arm. In today's world of transparency and citizen involvement, this is key to success. Ideally, a statutory spending limit will be replaced by a spending limit amendment to the Constitution.

To fully appreciate the power of this spending limit approach, one need only look at what might have happened over the past twenty years had a spending limit been in effect, versus the volatility of actual spending during that time. It would have imposed a limit on federal spending which would have prevented TARP, the stimulus, and the other spending that is currently breaking the bank.

- Spending reallocations within the limit: it is clear that some categories of spending—especially "entitlements"—will continue to grow, by their nature, until the reforms of Medicare, Social Security, and Medicaid (and other means-tested programs) can begin to take effect and restrain the growth of these programs. Meanwhile, to stay within the limit we must do two things:
  1. freeze spending in certain categories such as federal payroll and benefits; and
  2. reduce federal spending in a broad range of discretionary, as well as so-called "mandatory" (entitlements) programs by consolidating programs, terminating programs, reducing programs, and devolving programs to state and local governments.

Freeze Spending

- Freeze some federal spending: the first spending control step is to identify what current aspects of federal spending can be "frozen," and in being frozen, can be reduced as a share of a growing GDP over time. The immediate and obvious choice is the federal workforce, which has grown bloated and highly over-compensated in relationship to their counterparts in the private sector, especially during the belt-tightening of this recession. When we use the term "frozen," we mean that total expenditures for that category are held constant, although changes can occur within the mix of expenditures within that category.

■ Reduce the benefits for the federal workforce: we must control pensions, health, vacation, sick leave, etc., making them comparable to the private sector. In the past several years, the rate of growth in benefits inside government has far exceeded benefits in the private sector. This is largely because of labor union involvement at the state government level, but also in some cases at the federal level. On April 10, 2009, *USA Today* reported, "The pay gap between government workers and lower-compensated private employees is growing as public employees enjoy sizable benefit growth even in a distressed economy, federal figures show. Public employees earned benefits worth an average of $13.38 an hour in December 2008, the latest available data, the Bureau of Labor Statistics (BLS) says. Private-sector workers got $7.98 an hour."[3] On December 10, 2009, *USA Today* again reported, "Federal employees making salaries of $100,000 or more jumped from 14% to 19% of civil servants during the recession's first 18 months—and that's before overtime pay and bonuses are counted. Federal workers are enjoying an extraordinary boom time—in pay and hiring—during a recession that has cost 7.3 million jobs in the private sector."[4]

■ Restructure the government's workforce: it is a little noticed fact that the total number of federal employees in the executive branch of the federal government has barely moved since 1962. That year, the executive branch employed 2,485,000 civilian employees. In 2009, there were 2,774,000 employees. Including military, legislative, and judicial employees, the size of the federal bureaucracy has fallen from 5,354,000 in 1962 to 4,430,000 in 2009.[5] For those who think that is a good thing, consider that a stagnant government workforce over fifty years means there have been no great efficiencies. Likewise, much of the growth of the federal government is masked because state governments are forced to hire employees to administer federal programs. Consequently, state and local government employment is growing rapidly because of federal mandates. Restructuring programs, departments, and innovating could both decrease the size of the federal bureaucracy legitimately as well as help states and municipalities start downsizing.

Spending Reduction Principles

Reduce federal spending: we must reduce federal spending in all categories of the federal budget (mandatory and defense and non-defense discretionary programs) by following and employing these principles and tools:

- Get Washington out of business and stop competing with the private sector: the federal government has no authority or responsibility to run trains (AMTRAK), operate the air controller network and airports, produce power (Tennessee Valley Authority), or run any of the myriad of other businesses in which it is engaged.
- Washington (more precisely, all of us as taxpayers) should not be the debt guarantors of last resort. That is what we have been doing with Freddie Mac and Fannie Mae, so-called

government-sponsored enterprises (GSEs), which are now under federal conservatorship and represent a huge liability for United States taxpayers. The same holds for the Pension Benefit Guaranty Corporation,[6] by which taxpayers pick up the pieces after private-pension promises have been broken by unions and defunct companies. There must be no more "defined pension" programs, public or private, which can and do create long-term unfunded liabilities. Whatever an employer—public or private—owes to an employee for future benefits—pensions, healthcare, etc.—should be calculated and paid concurrently with the employee's paycheck into a 401k-type account owned exclusively by the individual (not a company or union fund), with no lingering (unfunded) liabilities.

Stop Subsidizing Providers of Service

Washington—and governments at all levels—should never subsidize the provider of services, only—if at all—the recipient of services. Consider that families on welfare are given money to use for the purchase of shelter, food, clothes, transportation and so on. That's the right way to do it if government is going to be involved in social safety-net activities. But, in addition, lobbying forces have been employed by business interests to create programs—ostensibly to help the poor—which provide direct payments and subsidies to the providers of goods and services. Let's look at a few examples:

■ The building industry and home-financing industry have lobbied for and backed creation of public housing, Section 8 housing, guaranteed mortgages, and more, all for their own benefit, getting direct subsidies from taxpayers. The housing debacle that set off and perpetuated this recession was partially caused by homebuilders who produced as many as 25 percent more homes than could have been absorbed during this last bubble, supported by Barney Frank, Freddie, Fannie, and Wall Street, whose programs and bonuses precipitated this disaster.

■ Agriculture lobbies have not been content with crop subsidies (we thought we had ended them with the 1996 Freedom to Farm Act) but have been the driving force behind programs, ostensibly for the poor, which subsidize the agricultural providers, not the poor: food stamps, school lunches, and numerous other food programs. The waste in these programs is growing worse, with students taking advantage of "free" food and wasting much of it.[7] Youth obesity problems are traceable to these programs.[8]

■ In the name of providing public transportation for the poor, we have wasted billions subsidizing costly fixed-rail systems and public buses all armed with wheelchair retrievers. Overpaid drivers, operators, and administrators run costs through the roof for cities, counties, and transit districts. It would be far cheaper to provide the poor with taxi fare that would encourage private jitney services to emerge, which with the use of cell phones, computer routers, and GPS systems could pick people up and deliver them from and to the precise places for which they need service. In any event, this cannot be done from Washington. It is entirely a local matter. Delivering local transportation dollars to Washington to be re-distributed back to the place of origin in a form unlikely to meet local needs is the ultimate folly of central planning.

■ Medicaid is the premier example of what happens when you subsidize the provider of services rather than the purchaser. Low-income citizens "served" by Medicaid are as in the dark regarding the costs and utilization of medical services as the rest of us who are stuck with third-party payers.

They never see the bills and have no reason not to overuse the system. Give them health savings accounts, funded directly, and let them become cost-conscious health services consumers incentivized by being rewarded with funds remaining at year's end.

■ The United States Department of Education spends $79 billion a year and doesn't educate one child, all the while subsidizing state and local education departments, teachers' unions, grant writers, specialists, and bureaucrats. Parents don't get a dime directly. Again, we subsidize the providers of often inferior educational products, rather than the purchasers (parents), who would make sure their kids got their money's worth. The Democrats and teacher union sycophants have recently helped de-fund the successful scholarship program in Washington, D.C., which has been a huge success in reforming the failed public school system in the nation's capitol.

Stop Funding Local Programs

Washington should do no funding of strictly state and local projects. It is absurd to route taxpayer money from Chicago, Los Angeles, or New York through Washington and back to those cities for projects that have no federal nexus whatever. And yet that is what we have been doing since 1974 in the Community Development Block Grant Program, now nearly $4 billion a year.[9] It is these kinds of programs that account for much of the absurd "earmarks," which have so riled—and properly so—taxpayers nationwide...and virtually incited tea partiers to take to the streets in protest. This program—and many others regularly receive an "ineffective," i.e., flunking grade, from the Office of Management and Budget.

If we were to follow this principle we would be virtually assured that we would see an end to purely local earmarks of the following kinds.

- $588,000 for a marina in Alexandria, Louisiana;
- $245,000 for the expansion of an art museum in Allentown, Pennsylvania;
- $147,000 for a canopy walk at the Atlanta botanical gardens in Georgia;
- $196,000 for expanding the Calvin Coolidge State historic site in Vermont;
- $294,000 for a community recreational facility in New Haven, Connecticut;
- $196,000 for the construction of an auditorium in Casper, Wyoming;
- $441,000 to replace a county exposition center in Umatilla, Oregon;
- $98,000 for the Pearl Fincher Museum of Fine Arts in Spring, Texas;
- $245,000 for renovations to awnings at a historical market in Roanoke, Virginia;
- $294,000 for the development of an educational program at the Houston Zoo in Texas.[10]

Washington should additionally not be operating programs that can and should be devolved to state and local governments using the '96 welfare reform block grant model. There are about 85 federal means-tested "entitlement" programs ripe for reorganization, consolidation, and devolution to the states/local governments through the use of finite block grants, eliminating federal rules and regulations, and leaving the operations and potential savings entirely in the hands of the locals.

The key program to block grant is Medicaid. Under the current matching grant system, states are encouraged to over-expand their Medicaid programs. With a block grant, states would be encouraged to cut waste and design more efficient programs.

Other principles that should guide reform include ensuring that the federal government should never pay more for the performance of a function or activity than a competitive market rate. Anything beyond that can honestly be said to be an improper "gift" of "public funds." To this end, all service and support functions should be out-sourced pursuant to competitive bids in the private sector, such as janitorial services, building maintenance, security (on non-military facilities), computer and electronic support, vehicle fleet maintenance, etc. Also, as soon as possible, we should repeal the 1931 Davis-Bacon Act that requires that "prevailing (union) wages"[11] be paid on all construction jobs funded by the federal government. The implementation of these two disciplines would save taxpayers billions.

To prove they belong to a party of solutions, Republicans should set forth their own budget and show how it can lead to spending reduction and balance within the next ten years or less. The Republican Study Committee (RSC) has done just that. It has emphasized many of the same guiding principles we have put forward for budgeting and to get us to balance in 2020.[12]

THE PLAN

The only way we can ever get to a balanced budget and reduce the size of government is to establish a 10-year plan or a "glide-path." With it, we can estimate the annual increments in the economic growth rate so we can more rapidly expand the size and strength of the United States economy.

Congress should start the right-sizing process by following its own rules regarding program authorization and the appropriation processes; if they did so, huge savings in expenditures would be made.

In the House, Rule XXI requires that if any appropriation is made for a program for which there is not a current authorization by the appropriate policy committee, a point of order will lie when the measure is brought to the floor of the House.[13] Any Member may assert the point of order, which then requires approval of a majority of the House to consider that discrete appropriation. CBO is required to report annually on the dollar value and names of the appropriations that would run afoul of this rule. For 2010, $290 billion of appropriations do not have a current authorization and would be subject to the point-of-order and up-or-down vote.[14] The programs in question include many of those we most love to hate, including Legal Services Corporation, the National Endowment for the Arts, and so many others that have not been reauthorized in the past fifteen to twenty years. How have they avoided this important up-or-down vote on the floor of the House? The House Rules Committee, even when controlled by Republicans, wrote a rule for the appropriation around the House rule so that a point of order would not lie.[15]

It is time Republicans used the House Rule XXI to their advantage. Control of the House in the 2010 election for purposes of imposing this rule would be justification enough. We have the potential of forcing up-or-down policy votes on these programs in the authorizing committees. This would put members on record, possibly voting for some of the worst programs in the history of Congress. If the bad guys win, we put a bull's-eye on their shirt for that vote; if they fail to authorize, we use the Rule XXI procedure to excise some of the worst, big-spending programs in Congress. It is a win-win for the good guys. Sure, the Left may win some of the point-of-order votes on the floor, but again they do so at great political risk to themselves; that is exactly what we should be aiming for.

- Oversight committees and sub-committees should identify programs for termination, consolidation, trimming or devolution. Congress should bite the bullet and start de-funding

the "low-hanging-fruit" programs that always get "ineffective" (or flunking) grades when OMB reviews them; collapse duplicative programs (like the dozens of training
programs in the Department of Labor) into a handful of the
ones found most effective; and devolve the operation of programs to the lowest levels of government. The House, which
has a standing Oversight and Government Reform Committee, and numerous oversight sub-committees, should
commence the process as soon as the House is in Republican hands. The leadership could instruct the policy and
appropriations committees to key on this oversight work.

■ Congress should create independent commissions to help
reduce the size of government. Congress can authorize the
creation of independent commissions, using the BRAC
model (see Chapter Ten: Downsize Government) to recommend packages of programs to terminate annually, subject
to a single up-or-down vote in both Houses or packages of
reductions that will automatically take place unless both
Houses reject the proposals by up-or-down votes. Multiple
commissions, to cover various functional areas of the government, may be the best approach, with annual recommendations over a three-year period. New commissions can
then be appointed to make it an on-going process. The
attractiveness of this approach is that one House of Congress, alone, can establish commissions to advise its Members and, through the appropriations process, simply
de-fund failing programs.

■ Non-government organizations and individuals can play a
key role in helping the independent commissions and Congress reduce the size of government. We know the power of
the Internet, social networking, and bloggers, when combined with information, availability, and transparency, can

influence policy and political outcomes. Chris Edwards and his team at the Cato Institute have created a website, "Downsizing the Federal Government,"[16] that is ready-made for getting the word out and educating people on these issues. The same holds true for Brian Reidl at Heritage,[17] Scott Hodge at the Tax Foundation, Inc.,[18] Traci Sharp and her State Policy Network (the state-based think tanks);[19] the several national taxpayer groups: Grover Norquist's Americans for Tax Reform,[20] Dick Armey and Matt Kidde's Freedom Works,[21] Duane Parde's National Taxpayers Union,[22] Tom Schatz's Citizens Against Government Waste,[23] our National Tax Limitation Committee;[24] and generalist conservative organizations such as the American Conservative Union,[25] Free Congress Foundation,[26] Americans for Prosperity[27] and, of course, all of the tea party organizations that have emerged nationwide.

CREATING A WEALTH WEDGE BY RIGHT-SIZING GOVERNMENT

We might identify this process as the creation of a "wealth wedge," as we move our Nation into the 4 to 6 percent annual economic growth rate change. If we do nothing, and allow Obama to continue spending and taxing us into oblivion, we will be stuck with his "stagnation wedge" as our national economic growth rate hovers at or just above zero. To visualize the difference, look at the chart we have prepared.

While we can't know for sure the rate of improvement in our economy, or the growth rate percentage in any particular year, the compounding effect will be staggering versus the big-spending Obama stagnation wedge. And every year of magnified growth creates a new and larger economic base from which our Nation can grow in the years following and produce more tax revenue even while tax rates are cut.

Let's assume Obama/Pelosi/Reid policies carried the day for ten years at an average 1 percent annual growth or less. That might generate an eight or ten percent increase in the size of the economy over ten years. But if we go on the right-sizing path, we may have an average of four-five percent growth compounded over 10 years, leading to an even higher sustainable growth level. The size of our economy could achieve a 50+ percent increase during that time period, with significantly greater tax revenues with which to meet entitlement and other demands. That is the impact of compound growth, which Albert Einstein once remarked is "the most powerful force on earth."

Creating a government of the right size will require a total overhaul of the tax code. Lindy L. Paull, who served as chief of staff for the Joint Committee on Taxation, told the Senate Finance Committee: "The Internal Revenue Code consists of nearly 1.4 million words and includes 693 separate sections that impact individual taxpayers. The Treasury Department has issued some 20,000 pages of regulations containing over 8 million words. Individual taxpayers who file an annual form 1040 must deal with its 79 lines, 144 pages of instructions and 11 schedules totaling 443 lines plus instructions to go with them. There are 19 separate worksheets embedded in the Form 1040

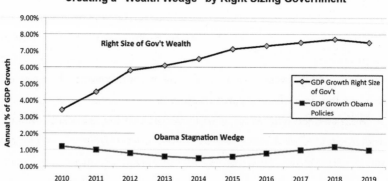

Creating a "Wealth Wedge" by Right Sizing Government

instructions, and the possibility of filing numerous other forms, depending on the circumstances."[28]

The Internal Revenue Service's national taxpayer advocate estimates that taxpayers spend $193 billion each year to comply with income tax requirements. This amounts to 14 percent of aggregate income tax receipts.[29]

Tax Freedom Day is the day you stop working for government and start working for yourself. In 1910 that day was January 19th, when just 5 percent of a person's income was taken in taxes.[30] One hundred years later, Tax Freedom Day is nearly three months later—April 9th (and later in higher-tax states)—when the tax take is 26 percent of a person's income. When you add indirect taxes and deficit spending, government is now spending nearly 40 percent of the nation's income (GDP).[31]

The federal corporate income tax, at 35 percent, is the second-highest among western nations.[32] When you add the state income tax, it is the highest. This is having a devastating effect on trying to hold and build businesses and jobs in the United States.

TAX UNCERTAINTY DEVASTATING

United States capital gains taxes are about to increase from 15 percent to 20 percent,[33] which will have a devastating effect on investments and United States venture capital. The death (estate) tax, which has fallen to zero this year (2010), is scheduled to jump to 55 percent in 2011 unless Congress acts to prevent it.[34] The uncertainties about these and other taxes and tax policies have kept economic recovery off balance and exacerbated the recession.

With all the uncertainty at this point regarding spending, deficits, and taxes, it is probably not wise to junk the current tax system for the "devil you don't know." Obama/Pelosi/Reid could well make it worse. What we do know is that we must be resolute in our opposition to their efforts to layer a new tax *on top of the federal income tax system*. They are beating the drums for a European-style Value Added Tax (VAT),[35] which is a hidden sales tax imposed on each step of the manufacturing and service-providing process. If we succumb to the liberal demands, we will make it nearly impossible to right-size government, because a VAT is an enormous engine of additional revenue and is largely invisible—just what socialists want.

NEW TAX SYSTEM?

It may be that the best solution is a flat-rate income tax—with the same rate applicable to personal as well as corporate earnings—at a low rate (say 10 percent) with few if any deductions, set-offs, or exceptions (i.e., eliminate home-mortgage interest, property tax, charitable and work-related expense deductions but keep off-sets for ordinary and necessary business expenses/deductions). It can be turned into a consumption-based tax if the tax is not imposed on any income that is saved or invested.

We would all like to see an end to the IRS. Uniformly, people resent its invasiveness and snooping, as well as the complexity of the code and vexing filing requirements. While repealing the income tax would help curb the IRS, so long as we have income-based Social Security, i.e., FICA; payments by both employees and employers, we have income-revealing filings. If, on the other hand, we converted Social Security to a means-tested program, we could choose a non-income-based source of revenue, while we transitioned workers from Social Security to a Chilean-style private retirement system.

We could then choose Senator Jim DeMint's fully consumption-based "8½ percent solution," with an 8½ percent federal retail sales tax and an 8½ percent VAT, but only if we have significant, tough-to-alter restraints on federal spending, including a federal spending limit to prevent rate creep with a VAT. Or we could choose the "Fair Tax," a straight federal retail sales tax (we need to make sure that the federal tax, when added to an existing state sales tax, is not so high that it assures creation of a significant "underground," or non-sales-tax paying, economy).

PRINCIPLES OF TAXATION

As we set America on a new spending course, in pursuit of a right-sized government, and have the luxury of converting to a new federal tax system, we should be guided by principles articulated by two of the wisest and most experienced free-market economists in America: Steve Entin and Larry Hunter. In their "A Framework for Tax Reform,"[36] they have provided an invaluable checklist for a sound tax system. Here is what they recommend, in part:

A sound system of taxation has two purposes:

1. Raising revenue to pay for government goods, services, and activities; and
2. "Pricing" government to let taxpayers know how much they are being charged for government goods and services so that, as voters, they may decide in an informed manner how much government activity they wish to support with their votes...

PRINCIPLES OF A SOUND TAX SYSTEM

Economic efficiency: To be sound, a tax system must be economically efficient, inflicting as little damage as possible on the economy.

Every tax system distorts economic decisions and leads to less economic activity than otherwise would occur, resulting in what economists call "deadweight loss." A sound tax system should be designed to minimize these losses...

Technical efficiency: A sound tax system should be technically efficient. It should impose on taxpayers the smallest possible compliance and preparation burdens, and should minimize the administrative and enforcement costs for the government...

Political efficiency: A sound tax system is politically efficient, distorting as little as possible voters' choices regarding the amount and the composition of public goods and services produced by the government and consumed by the public. It should also be a system that the public views as correct and is willing to support, allowing it to remain stable without constant churning and tinkering by government...

Neutrality: Tax "neutrality" means measuring income correctly and then levying taxes evenly, at equal rates, on all uses of income by all income producers. Defining income correctly results in an appropriate tax base. An even tax rate applied to that base without bias minimizes the distortion of economic activity and does the least damage to economic growth...

Visibility: "Visibility" means a tax system is transparent to the taxpayers so it is clear how much government costs and who is paying for it. Visibility is necessary for voters to determine effectively the amount and composition of government spending at which its benefits match its costs. Visibility is a key element in providing political efficiency...

Fairness: "Fairness" means equal treatment under the law, equal treatment for those equally situated, and no discrimination among taxpayers unequally situated unless that discrimination is consistent with the purposes and principles of a sound tax system...

Simplicity: "Simplicity" means a tax system is not unnecessarily complicated beyond what is required of it to be consistent with the purposes and principles of a sound tax system. Albert Einstein's general admonition to "make everything as simple as possible but not simpler" applies in particular to designing a sound tax system...

PRESERVING A STABLE TAX SYSTEM

If people and their elected representatives come to understand
the principles that define a sound tax system, and reach a consensus to implement such a system, then one would hope that
they would be reluctant to tamper with it. However, the
incentive to shift the tax burden onto others, or to hide the
true cost of government from the voters, may prove irre-
sistible. Therefore, legal or constitutional barriers that limit
the ability of political majorities to go beyond the two basic
purposes of a tax system may be required...

NOTE WHAT IS MISSING

Not one word of the above discusses using tax policy to affect social
policy. Article 1, Section 8, Clause 1 of the Constitution says, "The
Congress shall have Power To lay and collect Taxes, Duties, Imposts
and Excises, to pay the Debts and provide for the common Defence
and general Welfare of the United States." It clearly means taxation is
to bring in revenue to the federal treasury to pay for the operating
costs of the United States. Instead, Congress has chosen to use the burgeoning tax code as the chief vehicle for social change in the United
States. Republicans and Democrats are both guilty of it and both
should stop it.

Second, not one word of the above mentions "attacking the rich."
"Tax cuts for the rich" is the oft repeated mantra of the Democrats.
Punishing success should not be in our tax code. But it is also not even
true. The rich pay vastly more than the poor in our tax code and still
use their net income to innovate and create jobs. We should stop playing class warfare with a tax code.

Tax reform proposals should be judged on whether they will improve
the functioning of the economy, raise living standards, reduce compliance and enforcement costs, and promote better government. Reform

proposals that are designed with the principles and attributes mapped out above will have a far greater chance of leading to those outcomes than plans cobbled together with no vision and no guideposts.

COMMON-SENSE CITIZEN TESTS

In addition to government resources for evaluation of federal departments and programs, there are common-sense tests available to concerned, thoughtful citizens.

The first question to ask is whether a program in question oversteps the propriety of and need for government involvement in the area it addresses. A concerned citizen might ask whether any other entity besides the government can meet the needs an individual program purports to fulfill.

It is impractical for any individual, business organization or state and local government to defend the entire nation, engage in diplomatic interchange with foreign countries, provide international security, or any of our other vital national functions. These are clearly the province of a central government and are assigned to the federal government by the United States Constitution. So, too, are the printing of a common currency, providing for immigration and naturalization, and operating the federal justice system. Veterans' affairs, defense-related atomic energy and space exploration, federal-employee affairs, operations of Congress, the federal courts and the White House, and the tax-collection function are all inherently discharged only by a government national in scope. While certain planning aspects of an interstate road network and air transportation system may be appropriate functions of the federal government, the execution of the plan can be done privately or at some other level of government.

A review of the federal budget by function and sub-function suggests that the activities noted above exhaust the functions which a practical-necessity test would impose on the federal government.

The next question to consider is whether the federal government is constitutionally or contractually bound to perform the function under examination and, in performing it, does the federal government remain a neutral party or does it promote one set of values over another?

We can approach this test by considering two distinct questions:

1. What legal requirements underpin various federal functions?
2. What role does the federal government play in carrying out such functions?

In considering the first question, the range of legal requirements would seem to be:

a) A requirement imposed by the Constitution itself;
b) A requirement imposed by contract validly entered into between the federal government and others;
c) A requirement that is purely discretionary—it may be embodied in federal statute, but that statute may be repealed (or not renewed) at will.

With respect to the second question, the range of roles of the federal government with respect to its various programs would seem to be:

a) A role that is neutral—as a referee between competing interests;
b) A role that involves redistribution of wealth and income to activities that are largely ideologically neutral;
c) A role that involves financing programs that advance specific political, economic, social and philosophical ideas and values at the expense of others.

THE PERFORMANCE TEST

If it is appropriate and needed, impartially executed and constitutional, then the final question is whether it is performing effectively. Is there a clearly defined mission or set of goals, is there a plan to accomplish them, and is the program on task and making progress? Or has it lost its way, turning aside from or inappropriately expanding its mission and original purpose? Or even worse, is it seeking its own perpetuation as an end? Is it efficient and free of waste, fraud, and corruption, or is it intrinsically susceptible to abuse?

In *Meeting America's Economic Crisis: A "Road Map" to Emergency Federal Spending Reductions*, the 1981 book that the National Tax Limitation Committee distributed to senators and representatives, it offered performance criteria as a "road map" to establish priorities. Congress has given plenty of lip service to such recommendations, as it has to the Heritage Foundation's "Mandate for Leadership," Cato Institute's "Downsizing the Federal Government" recommendations, and to various special commissions' reports, but not much has been done to actually implement them.

The performance criteria, nevertheless, constitute another evaluative tool by which federal programs and activities can be compared and prioritized. The performance criteria are:

1. Proneness to fraud and abuse;
2. Proneness to error, inefficiency and waste;
3. Conflict or lack of coordination with other programs;
4. Failure to satisfy cost-benefit criteria;
5. Unjustified expansions of benefit eligibility;
6. Lack of uniform national benefit;
7. Impractical/unattainable program goals;
8. Programs best performed by state, local or private agencies.

TEST RESULTS: GOVERNMENT FAILS

Those federal functions and programs which fail to pass a responsible citizen's application of these tests should get an F—and be permanently kicked out of Washington.

CHAPTER 14

IS A NEW PARTY THE ANSWER?

It does not require a majority to prevail, but rather an irate, tireless minority keen to set brush fires in people's minds.[1]

—SAMUEL ADAMS

It is perfectly natural to say—as many tea partiers do—"clean house," "vote them all out," or "one party is no better than the other." There is no question but that over time many Republicans have thrown in with the enemies of the Republic, whether it be egregious earmarks, surrender to environmental hostage-taking, Wall Street bailouts, or a thousand other giveaways and capitulations.

But recent experiences with ObamaCare and other radical legislative proposals have drawn a clear line in the sand: Republicans in Congress have stood resolutely and uniformly for individual freedom, fiscal responsibility, and the Constitution, while virtually all Democrats—led by Constitution shredder-in-chief Barack Obama—have sold out our people and the nation. We don't need a new party, but we do need to make the Republican Party stronger, leaner, and meaner in the pro-America, pro-freedom, pro-Constitution, anti-debt-and-spending direction.

We can do this by using primary elections in open seats and winnable Democrat seats to nominate the strongest fiscal conservative among the candidates who can win in November. We have to be smart enough to know that you're unlikely to elect a Jim DeMint to the Senate in Maine or Minnesota, but you don't need to accept a Lindsey Graham in South Carolina or a Charley Crist in Florida. Fit the candidate to the state or district, but keep pushing the envelope in the fiscal-conservative, pro-Constitution-and-individual-freedom direction.

A "rebellion" party—or a new one by any other name—might feel good, but you won't win elections and you'll divide up our vote, putting the Democrats in office.

TEDDY ROOSEVELT & ROSS PEROT: 3RD PARTY CANDIDATES

On September 6, 1901, President William McKinley attended the Pan-American Exposition in Buffalo, New York. An assassin shot McKinley who, over the next few days, deteriorated and died.[2] On September 13, 1901, Theodore Roosevelt became President of the United States.

Roosevelt would serve until 1909. In 1908, Roosevelt decided not to seek office again, choosing instead to support William Taft. Roosevelt championed Taft as a "progressive" but ultimately decided Taft was not progressive enough.

In 1912, Roosevelt decided to run for office again as a Republican. President Taft defeated him in the Republican Primary. Undeterred, Roosevelt ran under the Progressive Party banner nicknamed the "Bull Moose Party." Combined, Taft and Roosevelt received 50.6 percent of the popular vote, but they were soundly defeated by President Woodrow Wilson with 41.8 percent of the vote.[3]

Theodore Roosevelt's progressive movement gave Woodrow Wilson victory.

Fast forward to 1992. The public had grown extremely disenchanted with both the Democrats and Republicans. H. Ross Perot, harnessing his billions of personal dollars, ran as an independent reform candidate from Texas against the incumbent, Republican George H. W. Bush, and Arkansas's Governor Bill Clinton, a Democrat.

Republicans were angry at George H. W. Bush for a variety of reasons most typically summed up in his breaking his "read my lips: no new taxes" pledge. Ironically, midway through Bush's presidency, with the success of the Gulf War, his presidential approval rating was higher than any other modern American President's approval, including Ronald Reagan's.

Voter love was fleeting for President Bush. Bill Clinton received 43.0 percent of the popular vote making him the 42nd President of the United States. Perot and Bush combined received 56.4 percent of the popular vote.[4]

1912 saw the most popular third-party candidate ever run for the presidency. Not only was he the most popular third-party candidate ever, he had also previously served as President of the United States and was at no loss for name recognition. Still, Teddy Roosevelt received only 27.4 percent of the popular vote.[5]

1992 saw the best funded third-party candidacy for President in the form of billionaire H. Ross Perot. Perot was able to harness both his billions and the anger and disenchantment of a bipartisan group of reform-minded voters to get 18.9 percent of the popular vote.[6]

If the most popular third-party candidate and the best funded third-party candidate can only succeed in getting Democrats elected to the White House, how exactly would 2010 be any different for congressional or senatorial races? For the answer, ask the nearest statewide elected Libertarian candidate. You can't. Such a person does not exist.

THE 2010 UPRISING

This is the reality in which we live—because of campaign finance laws, existing war chests, long-established party structures, and force of voter habit, among other things, we are a two-party nation.

In those states in which third-party candidates succeed (see Chapter 3's discussion on fusion), the third-party candidate rides the coattails of one of the major parties. Barack Obama, for example, ran as a New Party candidate in Illinois, but he also ran concurrently as a Democrat, leveraging the votes of both parties to win the Democratic nomination.

Tea party activists, conservatives, and reform-minded voters must work within the two-party system, whether they like it or not. The way to win is to fight in primaries.

In 2010, tea party activists around the country proved this point.

In Utah they became disenchanted with United States Senator Bob Bennett. Working from within the Utah Republican Party, tea party activists were able to defeat Bob Bennett at the Utah Republican Convention, sending Tim Bridgewater and Mike Lee into a primary. Conservatives then rallied to Mike Lee with Senator Jim DeMint leading the way. Lee won.[7]

In South Carolina, conservatives rallied to State Representative Nikki Haley. Working from within the Republican Party framework, activists from across the nation contributed to and volunteered for Nikki Haley, propelling her into first place and putting her into a runoff, which she won.[8]

In Florida, conservatives faced the anointed, handpicked, incumbent Governor of Florida. Establishment Republicans nationwide laid hands on Crist and declared him the chosen candidate. Conservatives said no thanks and rallied to former Florida Speaker Marco Rubio.

Endorsed by RedState.com in February of 2009, Rubio barely had a pulse. His poll numbers were under 8 percent with Crist over 50 percent.[9] Undeterred, South Carolina Senator Jim DeMint joined RedState as did Mike Huckabee and others. Rubio's support grew. By May of 2010, Charlie Crist had dropped out of the Republican primary to launch an independent bid that, as of this publication, appears to be failing.

In Kentucky, Republicans from Senator Minority Leader Mitch McConnell to former Vice President Dick Cheney endorsed Kentucky Secretary of State Trey Grayson.[10] Conservatives, however, rallied to Dr. Rand Paul, son of Congressman Ron Paul. Paul trounced Grayson in the Kentucky primary.

In Nevada, the establishment Republicans rallied to former Republican Party Chair Sue Lowden. Tea party activists initially split between businessman Danny Tarkanian and former Nevada Assemblywoman Sharron Angle. As the primary drew near, activists united behind Angle, sending her over the finish line and leaving establishment Republican heads spinning.

Again and again, working together, tea party activists have been able to come together and bring new blood into their political parties. They may not always be successful, but creating a third party would ensure defeat.

At the end of the day, there are real differences between the Republican and Democrat Parties. Sometimes voters feel they are choosing between the evils of two lessers, but that need not be the case if conservatives present compelling candidates and a compelling policy framework in primaries and win.

CONSERVATIVES CAN LEAD BY EXAMPLE

Fighting it out in the primaries to nominate the most conservative Republicans who can win in the fall is the proper way to strengthen and move the party in the right direction. But once the primary is behind us, if conservatives unite and demonstrate relentless commitment to electing the nominee, moderates can be held to the same standard. We can lead by example and demand no less of our more moderate brethren. Through this means we re-shape the party...in the right direction, avoiding the risks and travails of forging a new political party.

CHAPTER 15

TAKE BACK AMERICA

If you will not fight for the right when you can easily win without bloodshed, if you will not fight when your victory will be sure and not too costly, you may come to the moment when you will have to fight with all the odds against you and only a small chance of survival. There may even be a worse case: you may have to fight when there is no hope of victory, because it is better to perish than to live as slaves.[1]

—SIR WINSTON CHURCHILL

A tea party activist e-mailed RedState asking for advice on running for office. At the time, he lived in a town of 13,000 with a $29 million budget, an $8 million municipal payroll, and a $1 million deficit. He decided to put down the protest signs and pick up a campaign sign— his own. The advice back was simple.

Get a list of voters from the board of elections or your local political party. Put it in a spreadsheet and focus first on the people who have voted in the last two off-year elections.

Those are the likeliest to vote. Don't knock on every door—just the doors of likely voters.

Knock on as many doors as you can, and do it twice. Build your name ID up. Your message is simple: We can't sustain our government.

The hard part is not actually getting elected. The hard part is voting no on everything when you get in office. All your friends will tell you to vote no, but the moment it becomes about them and their pet projects they will turn on you. Well, some will at least, and it will make you mad.

Be prepared to vote no. And above all else, go into office planning to be there for one term and blow the place up. You do that and people will treat you as an honest broker, rewarding you with a second term. Don't go in to play it safe. Be bold.

It is a trite expression, but true nonetheless: freedom isn't free. Some people serve in the military fighting for our freedoms. Others get elected to office because they too feel compelled to fight in some way for freedom. The odds are against those freedom fighters who go into politics—more often than not, good people go in and get comfortable. It does not matter the party or beliefs. To proceed, we need men and women willing to fail, willing to take risks, willing to be thrown out of office for doing what is right.

In 2010, Democrat leaders finally realized there is no such thing as a permanent political majority, but there may still be a permanent policy victory. They forced through ObamaCare despite a majority of Americans not wanting it, daring the Republican Party to get rid of it.

Sure enough, many Republicans, including the House and Senate Republican leaders, talked about repeal, but caveated repeal with "replace the bad parts." Never mind that the Democrats structured ObamaCare so that no part can be removed without terrible economic consequences. But the Republican leadership was timid.

Not so the voters. Not so the tea party activists. Not so real conservatives. So we must fight, sometimes even within our particular political party.

The preceding chapters were about the why. Now you need to know the "for what end?" That end is freedom. And freedom comes by electing leaders who are committed to getting government out of the way. But to ensure we get the leaders we want, we must be willing to pick off incumbents, even in our own party, who are not committed to freedom.

LEARN THE RULES

In 2010, Utah Republican voters threw three-term Republican Senator Bob Bennett out of office. The whole movement was organized largely online and through tea party meetings around Utah.

The tea party activists figured out the Utah Republican convention rules. They organized for the Utah caucuses. They educated voters leading up to the caucuses, and they went into the caucuses with strength in numbers. A majority of the anti-Bennett voters became delegates to the state convention and Bennett went down quickly.

Two men were left standing after the convention. In Utah, if no one gets 60 percent of the vote in the convention, there is a primary. Businessman Tim Bridgewater and attorney Mike Lee went into the primary. Bennett endorsed Tim Bridgewater. It was the kiss of death. Mike Lee won in a close vote, moving Utah's senate seat dramatically to the right.

A few weeks after Mike Lee's victory, Bob Bennett gave an interview to PBS. The interview focused on the effort to oust him, and he gave this stunning quote:

> I found that a good many of the delegates simply wouldn't
> talk to me. They were so angry, so determined to—quote—
> "send Washington a message"—close quote—that coming to

one of my events to hear what I had to say on any of these things was—simply, they wouldn't do. **And many of them who did come, they would hold up their copy of the Constitution, and they would say, if it's not in the Constitution, you shouldn't do it. Well, I'm not quite ready to go that far in my conservative views.**[2] (Emphasis added)

What a stunning admission. A self-identified conservative Republican United States Senator from the solid Republican state of Utah is admitting that he is not willing to adhere to the Constitution as the parameters of his job.

Bob Bennett is just one example. To take out people like Bob Bennett, activists must learn the rules. That is extremely important. Though impolitic to say, the truth is many activists live in an idealized world and ignore or do not realize that there are real rules in politics that must be followed. Mastering the rules gives activists an advantage others do not have.

Tea party activists in Utah learned the rules of the Utah convention and beat a three-term incumbent Republican Senator.

TAKE BACK THE PARTY

In Maricopa County, AZ in the 2008 election cycle, there were 694,000 registered Republican voters. There are 6,231 precinct committeemen positions for the Republican Party in Maricopa County. Of those, only 1,989 were filled by February of 2009. In other words, one-third of the precinct committeemen positions were filled. More bluntly, three-tenths of one percent of the registered Republicans in Maricopa County, AZ were actively engaged in their party.[3]

In February of 2009, 200 people showed up at a tea party protest in Maricopa County. Assume, if you will, that half are not actively involved in the local Republican Party. That makes 100 people who were so hacked off at out-of-control government that they showed up at noon on a weekday to protest.

If those 100 people each became a precinct committeemen, they would have enough impact to make significant changes in the Maricopa County Republican Party. Why? Because of the nearly 2,000 named committeemen, not all are actively engaged. And of those who are, not all can show up at a meeting because of schedule conflicts.

Just 100 people.

Remember that 300 Spartans held off the Persian Army. Small numbers compared to the thousands of well armed Persians. Small numbers working well together can be powerful numbers. It just takes some dedication.

If we are to fundamentally change this country, we will do so through the existing party apparatus. And it is damn easy if you work at it with some friends. Think about the numbers. Take, as another example, Bibb County, Georgia. If you show up at a precinct meeting, you are probably going to become precinct captain because no one shows up. Then you have a good chance of becoming Area Captain because, again, few show up.

If you do it with your friends, pretty soon you are bringing your delegates to the county convention and picking your county chairman who then gets to have a say at the state level. Better yet, if you coordinate with like-minded citizens in other parts of your state, pretty soon you'll control your state party.

Then you have real power.

Ever hear of the "Butterfly effect?" To quote wikipedia, "Small variations of the initial condition of a dynamical system may produce large variations in the long-term behavior of the system."[4] You know it better as a butterfly flapping its wings in Japan causes a storm in California. Put in more relevant context—you showing up at your county Republican Party meeting causes a wholesale, long-term readjustment in the Republican Party.

Friends, we can't spend all day complaining about the state of our country and the state of the GOP. You don't have to invest your money, just your time and talent.

We need a lot less preaching and a whole lot more doing. The power of small numbers of people willing to show up at a political party meeting gets amplified over time. If you are willing, you and your like-minded friends can take over and change the Republican Party.

FIGHT FOR FREEDOM[5]

Once activists have taken over, they have to present a compelling plan of governance. They have to set up an agenda that makes long-term gains for freedom, not short-term gains to secure election. In short, the future leaders of the tea party generation must be prepared to sacrifice even some of their goals in the name of greater freedom of choice for everyone to live their own lives—the "leave me the hell alone" agenda, if you will.

The Republican Party has always embraced a wide range of ideological beliefs—and this diversity of thought has sometimes inspired conflict, as it has also led to great achievement. Yet through all debates, despite all regional or political concerns, the foundation of Republicanism has been the same since its inception: the freedom of the individual, and the value of every human life.

These principles have guided the party from its origin as a political force to destroy slavery, to the long fight against communism, to the ongoing battle for the sanctity of the unborn, to the present war against the forces of Islamism. Those principles will guide the Republican Party through the twenty-first century, and beyond. And we believe the GOP must rededicate itself to the idea of individual freedom—of being the party that believes not in government mandated parity, which wields the power of the bureaucracy to force a false equality of outcome, but in a level playing field for all Americans regardless of race, class, or creed—ensuring an equal opportunity to compete, succeed, and thrive.

The Republican Party must reclaim its rightful mantle as the leading champion of Freedom of Choice. People must be free to decide how to direct their lives for themselves, and then be responsible for their choices.

On education, Republicans believe you must be free to choose how you want to educate your children. Government should not stand in the way of your choice, whether in the form of home schooling, government schooling, charter schools, vouchers to leave a failing school for a thriving school, or other opportunities.

On healthcare, Republicans should embrace an end to regulatory regimes that prevent citizens from buying healthcare across state lines or otherwise disciplinary healthcare costs. Republicans should embrace reforms that allow the free market to play a greater role in healthcare, not a lesser role. Republicans should embrace total portability of healthcare so workers can be free to choose a new job without fear of losing their doctor or healthcare of their choice.

On taxes, Republicans should embrace the Republican Study Committee plan for an alternate flat tax. If you want to go through the regular 1040 process with itemized deductions, etc., do it. If you want to bypass that route, file a postcard return based on a flat tax—make it the taxpayer's choice en route to ending the income tax system altogether.

On energy, Republicans, including our presidential nominees, should embrace every option. You want nuclear power? Republicans should favor that choice. You want to use the resources we have instead of buying it from our enemies? Republicans should support legislation to allow us to drill here and now. You want methanol and other biofuels? Republicans should break down trade barriers that prevent the importation of ethanol and Republicans should kill subsidies that raise the price of food stuffs in the name of producing corn-based ethanol and other biofuels. Republicans should be in favor of letting consumers decide which light bulbs consumers want for their own homes.

On Social Security, Republicans should favor greater investment options for individuals' retirements such as the successful Chilean model. If an individual wants to keep the current social security regime, we should let them. If an individual wants greater control investing their social security, we should let them have it. And above all else, because the government has already made certain choices regarding social security and medicare withholdings, Republicans should not use FICA/FUTA revenues for anything but social security and medicare/Medicaid payments respectively, in the current year.

When individuals are allowed to choose for themselves, they take an ownership interest in their choices. One of the greatest failures of the present Republican leadership in Washington has been not aggressively communicating and supporting the the idea of an ownership society, which contains at its core the revolutionary undercurrent that motivated America's founding: that each individual holds within themselves the capacity and right to self-government.

This is an enormous contrast with the Democrats. In almost every area of their agenda, they are opposed to self-government. They advocate less freedom for the individual to direct their lives—they remove the freedom of choice from the American citizen, and give it instead to bureaucracies and agencies and the many eddies and tidepools of the federal government, all managed with the efficiency and responsibility of your local Department of Motor Vehicles.

Blogger Jon Henke, writing at thenextright.com in 2008, pointed out a blog post by progressive activist Chris Bowers.[6] This is the agenda the Left is openly willing to brag about and that, in Barack Obama's time in office the Left has championed. On the whole, the Left's causes include:[7]

■ crippling a worker's right to decide whether or not to join a union

- crippling a business's right to decide what salary an employee should be paid
- crippling an individual's right to decide on healthcare options outside the government
- crippling the ability of the military to defend the country abroad
- Crippling free speech in radio
- crippling rights to own a gun and defend yourself
- crippling the freedom to practice your religion without government interference
- crippling the ability of the United States to grow economically outside of government mandates.

In fact, Democrats are openly excited about nationalizing key American industries, from energy to healthcare to automobiles. Forget the free market—forget the capitalistic economy that made the country the envy of the world—in this area as in all others, the Democrats oppose the freedom of choice in directing your life.

Well, all areas but one. The only significant choice the Democrats will defend for an individual is to have the power to determine whether or not to destroy the life of an unborn child.

This is their only claim to the language of choice. It is a false claim. We do not believe this is a valid choice to be made, nor ever has in the course of human history, because it enables the purposeful destruction of innocent life. Where once the pro-abortion Left could make their argument based on ignorance of the process of human development, we now know the only choice the Democrats advocate is one that in almost every case kills a feeling, thinking American at its youngest and most vulnerable stage of life, whose only crime is one of inconvenience.

We believe in Individual Freedom of Choice—preserving the individual's right to life, liberty, and the pursuit of happiness—where the Left's agenda is to cripple the individual's freedom to choose, and replace it with dependence on government.

This is not new, but it is what we will have should the Democrats continue to increase in power. The Republican Party should not be shy about fighting to give people choices, regardless of whether the Democrats claim to be the "pro-choice" party when they are, in fact, only supporting choices made for death, and state control of everything else of importance.

It is time for the GOP to push forward expanding choices for individuals and families to give them a greater stake in their lives and provide them ownership of their life as a whole. It is time to pose this question to the American people: who should have the power to choose the path for your life, for your family? To choose where you receive healthcare, where your children learn, and where your tax dollars go? Should it be the self-appointed elite, intent on building a perfect society, because they know what is best for the communal citizenry? Or should it be you, with your own goals in mind, for the simple reason that you are an American?

This nation is at a tipping point. We will either go toward more government control of our lives, which is what the Left wants, or less government control of our lives. When people have the power to direct their own lives, government will shrink—and it will be hard, once an individual has control of his own life, to cede this control back to Washington. This generation of conservative political activists must unite to take back the Republican Party and use it as a vehicle to elect conservatives committed to freedom. From there, Republicans in government should fight to expand our choices, so we can take greater control of our lives. We believe in Freedom of Choice.

MALO PERICULOSAM, LIBERTATEM QUAM QUIETAM SERVITUTEM
"I prefer the tumult of liberty to the quiet of servitude."[8]
—Thomas Jefferson

ERICK ERICKSON
ACKNOWLEDGEMENTS

Throughout the course of writing this book, there are a number of people who I specifically wish to acknowledge and thank.

My wife and children, who let me stay up way past bedtime to write and my parents and in-laws for their support.

My co-author, Lew Uhler, and the National Tax-Limitation Committee, for their tireless work.

The front page contributors at RedState who helped collect notes and tidbits and keep the lights on when I cannot.

The readers of RedState, who inspired me throughout this process and kept saying, "You've got to write this book."

The men of the Dead Theologian Society, which is the fancy name for my bible study—I never have been without their prayers through this endeavor.

The Republican Study Committee, along with Senator Jim DeMint and Congressman Mike Pence's staffs, who made a great sounding board, along with the Senator and Congressman's various policy proposals.

Rush Limbaugh, who has been a willing and invaluable source of advice, friendship, and encouragement, not to mention inspiration to me five days a week for the last eighteen years since I first heard him on a father-son road trip to check out colleges.

Cato and the Heritage Foundation, both of which provided invaluable research and data.

The Hancock Committee for the States and American Majority for sending me all around the country to speak at events with local tea party activists to really appreciate the mood of country as I focused on this project.

Freedom fighters everywhere both inside and outside the tea party movement.

And most especially, Ben Domenech, Mike Krempasky, Josh Treviño, and Clayton Wagar, but for whom I would not be in a position to write this book, and that small band of brothers who must remain nameless, but on whom I rely every single day for wisdom, grace, and strength.

—Erick Erickson

LEWIS K. UHLER
ACKNOWLEDGEMENTS

There are many who have contributed to the message of this book. Their insights have proven invaluable, and I want to acknowledge their contributions. First of course is my co-author, Erick Erickson, who has been a delight to work with. Also, Tad DeHaven, Chris Edwards, Steve Entin, Stan Evans, John Fund, Larry Hart, Ted Hart, Larry Hunter, David A. Keene, Art Laffer, Dan Mitchell, Steve Moore, Michael New, William A. Niskanen, Barry Poulson, Richard Rahn, Congressman Paul Ryan, Bill Shaker, Richard Vedder, Jonathan Williams, Walter Williams, and the late Bob Carleson and Gerald Scully.

A special thanks to our Publisher, Regnery, Editor in Chief Harry Crocker, Editor Anneke Green, our National Tax Limitation Committee assistants, staff members and consultants: Owen Frisbee, Lisa Hart, Alan Osterstock, Ed Ring, Diane Sekafetz, and Jan Sowell.

NOTES

INTRODUCTION

1. "The Honduras Mess," *Wall Street Journal*, September 23, 2009; available at: http://online.wsj.com/article/NA_WSJ_PUB:SB10001 42405297020448830457442740398511889 2.html [accessed July 29, 2010].
2. "Uptick in Violence Forces Closing of Parkland Along Mexican Borders to Americans," FOXNews.com, June 16, 2010; available at: http://www.foxnews.com/us/2010/06/16/closes-park-land-mexico-border-americans/ [accessed July 29, 2010].

CHAPTER 1

1. "First Inaugural Address." The Public Papers of President Ronald W. Reagan. Ronald Reagan Presidential Library; available at: http://www.reagan.utexas.edu/archives/speeches/1981/12081a.htm [accessed August 2, 2010].
2. Fred Barnes, "Big Government Conservatism," *Weekly Standard*, August 18, 2003; available at: http://www.weeklystandard.com/Content/Public/Articles/000/000/003/017wgfhc.asp [accessed July 27, 2010].
3. Editorials, "Big Government Conservatives," *Washington Post*, August 15, 2005; available at: http://www.washingtonpost.com/

wp-dyn/content/article/2005/08/14/AR2005081400905.html [accessed July 27, 2010].

4. Jeffrey Gayner, "The Contract With America: Implementing New Ideas in the U.S.," Heritage Foundation, October 12, 1995; available at: http://www.heritage.org/Research/Lecture/The-Contract-with-America-Implementing-New-Ideas-in-the-US [accessed July 27, 2010].

5. "Republican Contract with America," U.S. House of Representatives; available at: http://www.house.gov/house/Contract/CON TRACT.html [accessed July 27, 2010].

6. Edward H. Crane, "On My Mind: GOP Pussycats," CATO, November 13, 2000; available at: http://www.cato.org/pub_dis play.php?pub_id=4463 [accessed July 27, 2010].

7. "75% Say Free Markets Better Than Government Management of Economy, Political Class Disagrees," Rasmussen Reports, July 23, 2010; available at: http://www.rasmussenreports.com/public_con tent/politics/general_politics/july_2010/ 75_say_free_markets_better_than_government_management_of_e conomy_political_class_disagrees [accessed July 27, 2010].

8. Shailagh Murray, "Republican lawmakers gird for rowdy tea-party," *Washington Post*, July 18, 2010; available at: http:// www.washingtonpost.com/wp-dyn/content/article/2010/07/17/ AR2010071702375.html [accessed July 27, 2010].

9. Halimah Abdullah, "Mitch McConnell, facing re-election battle, defends his record," McClatchy, October 21, 2008; available at: http://www.mcclatchydc.com/2008/10/21/54556/mitch-mcconnell-facing-re-election.html [accessed July 27, 2010].

10. Shailagh Murray, "Republican lawmakers gird for rowdy tea-party," *Washington Post*, July 18, 2010; available at: http:// www.washingtonpost.com/wp-dyn/content/article/2010/07/17/ AR2010071702375.html [accessed July 27, 2010].

11. Robert Schmidt, "Rick Renzi, Republican Congressman, Indicted by U.S.," Bloomberg, February 22, 2008; available at: http://

www.bloomberg.com/apps/news?pid=newsarchive&sid=abww0 wdvkvmu [accessed July 27, 2010].

12. Susan Schmidt and James V. Grimaldi, "Ney Pleads Guilty on Corruption Charges," *Washington Post*, October 14, 2006; available at: http://www.washingtonpost.com/wp-dyn/content/article/2006/10/13/AR2006101300169.html [accessed July 27, 2010].

13. Ibid.

14. Matthew 7:1–3, King James Version.

15. Alexis de Tocqueville, *Democracy in America* (Chicago: University of Chicago Press, 2000).

16. "Bush Says sacrificed free market principles to save economy," Breitbart; available at: http://www.breitbart.com/article.php?id=081216215816.8g97981o [accessed July 27, 2010].

17. Senate Session, "Paul Wellstone Mental Health and Addiction Equity Act of 2008 Continued," C-SPAN, October 1, 2008; video available at: http://c-spanvideo.org/videoLibrary/clip.php?appid=595262404 [accessed July 27, 2010].

18. "Fact Sheet: America's Expanding Ownership Society: Expanding Opportunities," WhiteHouse.gov, June 17, 2004; available at: http://georgewbush-whitehouse.archives.gov/news/releases/2004/08/20040809-9.html [accessed July 27, 2010].

19. Ibid.

20. "President's Remarks to the National Association of Home Builders," WhiteHouse.gov, October 2, 2004; available at: http://georgewbush-whitehouse.archives.gov/news/releases/2004/10/20041002-7.html [accessed August 4, 2010].

21. "Text: President Bush's Acceptance Speech to the Republican National Convention," *Washington Post*, September 2, 2004; available at: http://www.washingtonpost.com/wp-dyn/articles/A57466-2004Sep2.html [accessed July 28, 2010].

22. The Sarbanes–Oxley Act of 2002 (Pub.L. 107-204)

23. Allison Fass, "One Year Later, The Impact of Sarbanes Oxley," *Forbes*, July 22, 2003; available at: http://www.forbes.com/2003/

07/22/cz_af_0722sarbanes.html [accessed July 28, 2010].

24. Michael S. Malone, "Washington is Killing Silicon Valley," *Wall Street Journal*; available at: http://online.wsj.com/article/ SB122990472028925207.html [accessed July 28, 2010].

25. International Business Law Committee, "Unintended Consequences? The Effect of Sarbanes Oxley on Global Capital Markets," ABA Spring Meeting, March 17, 2007; available at: http:// www.abanet.org/buslaw/newsletter/0058/materials/pp8.pdf [accessed July 28, 2010].

26. Energy Policy Act of 2005 (Pub.L. 109-58)

27. Marianne Stigset, "Ethanol Drives Up Food Commodity Prices Datagro Says," Bloomberg, November 2, 2006; available at: http:/ /www.bloomberg.com/apps/ news?pid=newsarchive&refer=news&sid=ayonmpI2Y1dA [accessed July 28, 2010].

28. "Republicans Drunk on Ethanol," *National Review* Online, October 12, 2007; available at: http://article.nationalreview.com/ 330345/republicans-drunk-on-ethanol/the-editors [accessed July 28, 2010].

29. John Frydenlynd, "The Erosion of Freedom to Farm," Heritage Foundation, March 8, 2002; available at: http://www.heritage.org/ Research/Reports/2002/03/The-Erosion-of-Freedom-to-Farm [accessed July 28, 2010].

30. Ronald Utt, "The Bridge to Nowhere: A National Embarrassment," Heritage Foundation, October 20, 2005; available at: http://www.heritage.org/Research/Reports/2005/10/The-Bridge-to-Nowhere-A-National-Embarrassment [accessed July 30, 2010].

31. "Lott Says He's 'Damn Tired' of Porkbusters, Defends His Railroad to Nowhere," Tapscott's Copy Desk; available at: http://tapscottscopydesk.blogspot.com/2006/04/ lott-says-hes-damn-tired-of.html [accessed July 28, 2010].

32. For example, see, "Gulf War: Bush-Thatcher phone conversation (no time to go wobbly)," Margaret Thatcher Foundation; avail-

able at: http://www.margaretthatcher.org/document/110711 [accessed July 30, 2010].

33. Ronald Utt, "Federal Highway Program Shortchanges Half of the States," Heritage Foundation, April 15, 2010; available at: http://www.heritage.org/Research/Reports/2010/04/Federal-Highway-Program-Shortchanges-Half-of-the-States [accessed August 4, 2010].

34. Al Pessin, "China Increasing Military Ties in Latin America as Law Restricts US Military," GlobalSecurity.org, March 16, 2006; available at: http://www.globalsecurity.org/wmd/library/news/china/2006/china-060315-voa01.htm [accessed July 28, 2010].

35. Sir Winston Churchill, *The Second World War, Vol. 1: The Gathering Storm* (Mariner Books, 1986), 348.

36. U.S. Congress. Senate. *S.Amdt. 2786 to H.R. 3590 (Patient Protection and Affordable Care Act) Roll Call* Votes 111th Cong., 1st sess., 2009; available at: http://senate.gov/legislative/LIS/roll_call_lists/roll_call_vote_cfm.cfm?congress=111&session=1&vote=00389 [accessed August 2, 2010].

37. U.S. Congress. Senate. *S.391 Healthy Americans Act* Bill Summary & Status 111th Cong.; available at: http://thomas.loc.gov/cgi-bin/bdquery/z?d111:s.00391: [accessed August 2, 2010].

38. Too often, Republicans have favored comprehensive solutions to issues from financial reform to immigration to healthcare. Instead of simply securing the American border with Mexico, Republicans proposed a comprehensive solution that went nowhere. Republicans should be as wary of Republican comprehensivism as they are Democratic comprehensivism.

39. A discharge petition is a procedural mechanism in the U.S. House of Representatives that forces the Speaker of the House to hold a vote on a piece of legislation if 218 members of congress sign a "discharge petition" demanding a vote on designated legislation.

40. *McConnell v. Federal Election Commission*, 540 U.S. 93 (2003).

41. "Department of Homeland's Security Executive Staffing Project,"

National Academy of Public Administration, October 16, 2007; available at: http://www.napawash.org/pc_management_studies/ dhs.html [ACCESSED JULY 28, 2010].

42. "A Time For Choosing." Pre-Presidential Speeches. Ronald Reagan Presidential Library; available at http://www.reagan.utexas. edu/archives/reference/timechoosing.html [accessed August 2, 2010]

CHAPTER 2

1. Jonah Goldberg, *Liberal Fascism* (Doubleday, 2008).

2. Ibid.

3. *American Recovery and Reinvestment Act*, HR 1, 111th Congress, 1st sess.

4. Ibid.

5. "State of the Union 2010: President Obama's Speech," ABC News, January 27, 2010; available at: http://abcnews.go.com/Politics/ State_of_the_Union/state-of-the-union-2010-president-obama-speech-transcript/story?id=9678572 [accessed July 29, 2010].

6. Ibid.

7. "Track the Money," Recovery.Gov, Data generated on July 29, 2010; available at: http://www.recovery.gov/Pages/home.aspx [accessed July 29, 2010].

8. Peter S. Goodman, "Jobless Rate Falls to 9.7%, Giving Hope Worst Is Over," *New York Times,* February 5, 2010; available at: http://www.nytimes.com/2010/02/06/business/economy/ 06jobs.html [accessed July 29, 2010].

9. Christina Romer and Jared Bernstein, "The Job Impact of the Recovery and Reinvestment Plan," January 9,2009; available at: http://www.economy.com/mark-zandi/documents/The_Job_Impact _of_the_American_Recovery_Reinvestment_Plan.pdf [accessed August 2, 2010].

10. 10. Bureau of Labor Statistics, Department of Labor, "Labor Force Statistics from the Current Population Survey": available at: http://data.bls.gov/PDQ/servlet/SurveyOutputServlet?data_tool=lat

est_numbers&series_id=LNS14000000 [accessed August 2, 2010].

11. Comments made by Tom Harkin, *Andrea Mitchell Reports*, MSNBC, March 4, 2010; video reproduced at: http://tpm-livewire.talkingpointsmemo.com/2010/03/harkin-gop-threats-to-run-against-health-care-are-reverse-psychology.php [accessed July 29, 2010].

12. Robert Pear, "Changing Stance, Administration Now Defends Insurance Mandate as a Tax," *New York Times*, July 16, 2010; available at: http://www.nytimes.com/2010/07/18/health/policy/18health.html?_r=1.[accessed July 29, 2010].

13. Ibid.

14. Mary Katherine Ham, "It's Come to This: Obamacare Threatens White Castle," *Weekly Standard,* July 6, 2010; available at: http://weeklystandard.com/blogs/its-come-obamacare-threatens-white-castle. [accessed July 29, 2010].

15. Neil deMause, "IRS starts mopping up Congress's tax-reporting mess," CNNMoney.com, July 9, 2010; available at: http://money.cnn.com/2010/07/09/smallbusiness/irs_1099_flood/ [accessed July 29, 2010].

16. Pub. L. No. 111–48, Title IX, Subtitle A, § 9006 (2010).

17. National Taxpayer Advocate, "Report to Congress: Fiscal Year 2011 Objectives," Internal Revenue Service, June 30, 2010; available at: http://www.irs.gov/pub/irs-utl/nta2011objectivesfinal.pdf. [accessed July 29, 2010].

18. Z. Byron Wolf and Huma Kahn, "Bill Clinton Visits Capitol Hill to Rally Democrats on Healthcare," ABC News, November 10, 2009; available at: http://abcnews.go.com/Politics/HealthCare/bill-clinton-pushes-senate-democrats-health-care/story?id=9044652 [accessed July 29, 2010].

19. Brian Riedl, "Federal Spending by the Numbers 2010," Heritage Foundation, June 1, 2010; available at: http://www.heritage.org/research/reports/2010/06/federal-spending-by-the-numbers-2010 [accessed July 29, 2010].

20. Kiki Bradley and Robert Rector, "How President Obama's Budget Will Demolish Welfare Reform," Heritage Foundation, February 25, 2010; available at: http://www.heritage.org/Research/Reports/ 2010/02/How-President-Obamas-Budget-Will-Demolish-Welfare-Reform [accessed August 4, 2010].

21. Loren Heal, "New Federal Subsidies Marred by Marriage Penalty," National Center for Policy Analysis, July 6, 2010; available at: http://www.ncpa.org/media/new-federal-subsidies-marred-by-marriage-penalty-the-heartland-institute [accessed July 29, 2010].

22. Kathryn Nix, "Side Effects: Stay Single and Save 15 percent or More on Health Insurance," Heritage Foundation, May 3, 2010; available at: http://blog.heritage.org/2010/05/03/side-effects-stay-single-and-save-15-percent-or-more-on-health-insurance/ [accessed July 29, 2010].

23. Eamon Javers, "Inside Obama's bank CEOs meeting," *Politico,* April 3, 2009; available online at: http://www.politico.com/news/ stories/0409/20871.html [accessed July 29, 2010].

24. Johan Norberg, "Financial Fiasco: How America's Infatuation with Home Ownership and Easy Money Created the Economic Crisis," Cato Institute, 2009.

25. Associated Press, "Fannie Mae wants another $8.4B bailout," May 11, 2010; available at: http://www.gazettenet.com/2010/05/ 11/fannie-mae-wants-another-84b-bailout [accessed July 29, 2010].

26. "Fannie Mae seeks $8.4 billion after loss," *Washington Times*, May 11, 2010; available at: http://www.washingtontimes.com/ news/2010/may/11/fannie-mae-seeks-84-billion/?page=2 [accessed August 5, 2010].

27. Lindsay Renick Mayer, "Update: Fannie Mae and Freddie Mac Invest in Lawmakers," OpenSecrets.org, September 11, 2008; available at: http://www.opensecrets.org/news/2008/09/update-fannie-mae-and-freddie.html [accessed July 29, 2010].

28. Serena Ng and Thomas Catan, "We Were Prudent: AIG Man at Center of Crisis," *Wall Street Journal*, July 1, 2010; available at: http://online.wsj.com/article/ NA_WSJ_PUB:SB10001424052748703426004575338640175139822.html [accessed July 29, 2010].

29. Matt Cover, "Financial Reform Bill Passed by House Would Create 'Office of Minority and Women Inclusion' in Every U.S. Financial Regulatory Agency," CNSNews.com, July 12, 2010; available at: http://www.cnsnews.com/news/article/69215 [accessed July 29, 2010].

30. David Cho, Jia Lynn Yang, and Brady Dennis, "Lawmakers Guide Dodd-Frank bill for Wall Street reform into homestretch," *Washington Post*, June 26, 2010; available at: http://www.washington post.com/wp-dyn/content/article/2010/06/25/AR2010062500675. html [accessed July 29, 2010].

31. Patrice Hill, "American Reliance on Government at an All Time High," *Washington Times*, March 1, 2010; available at: http:// www.washingtontimes.com/news/2010/mar/01/americans- reliance-on-government-at-all-time-high/ [accessed July 29, 2010].

32. William Beach and Patrick Tyrrell, "The 2010 Index of Depend- ence on Government: Dramatic Spike in Dependence Projected," Heritage Foundation, June 28, 2010; available at: http:// www.heritage.org/Research/Reports/2010/06/The-2010-Index-of- Dependence-on-Government-Dramatic-Spike-in-Dependence-Pro- jected [accessed July 29, 2010].

33. Michael Greenstone and Adam Looney, "June's Employment Numbers Highlight America's Increasingly Distressed Communities," Brookings Institute, July 2, 2010; available at: http:// www.brookings.edu/opinions/2010/0702_jobs_greenstone.aspx [accessed July 29, 2010].

34. Hillary Clinton, Secretary's Remarks, "Situation in Honduras," U.S. Department of State, June 28, 2009; available at: http://www.state.gov/secretary/rm/2009a/06/125452.htm [accessed August 5, 2010].

35. "Remarks by the President on a New Beginning," White-House.gov, June 4, 2009; available at: http://www.whitehouse.gov /the_press_office/Remarks-by-the-President-at-Cairo-University-6-04-09/ [accessed August 4, 2010]

36. Remarks By President Obama And President Lee Myung-Bak Of The Republic Of Korea In Joint Press Availability." White-House.gov, June 16, 2009; available at: http://www.whitehouse. gov/the_press_office/Remarks-by-President-Obama-and-President-Lee-of-the-Republic-of-Korea-in-Joint-Press-Availability/ [accessed August 4, 2010].

37. Winston Churchill, "The Sinews of Peace," NATO/OTAN Online Library; available at: http://www.nato.int/docu/speech/1946/s 460305a_e.htm [accessed July 29, 2010].

38. Tom Baldwin, "Churchill bust casts shadow over special relation-ship with U.S.," *The Times*, January 31, 2009; available at: http:/ /www.timesonline.co.uk/tol/news/world/us_and_americas/arti-cle5622197.ece [accessed July 29, 2010].

39. Ibid.

40. Stephanie Griffith, "Outrage in Washington over Obama's Japan bow," AFP, November 16, 2009; available at: http://www.google. com/hostednews/afp/article/ALeqM5gVGYMxyEpqIynr98qF-CA 9ptFp6w [accessed August 5, 2010]. "Another Obama 'bow' flap," *USAToday*, April 13, 2010; available at: http://www.usa today.com/communities/theoval/post/2010/04/another-obama-b ow-flap/1 [accessed August 5, 2010].

41. Ben Smith, "White House: No bow to Saudi," *Politico*, April 8, 2009; available at: http://www.politico.com/blogs/bensmith/ 0409/ White_House_No_bow_to_Saudi.html [accessed August 5, 2010].

42. The Prowler, "Obama In Rude Denial," *The American Spectator*, March 29, 2010; available at: http://spectator.org/archives/2010/ 03/29/obama-in-rude-denial [accessed August 5, 2010].

43. Tim Shipman, " Barack Obama 'too tired' to give proper Welcome to Gordon Brown," *UK Telegraph*, March 7, 2009; available at:

http://www.telegraph.co.uk/news/worldnews/northamerica/usa/
barackobama/4953523/Barack-Obama-too-tired-to-give-proper-
welcome-to-Gordon-Brown.html [accessed July 29, 2010].

44. Ibid.

45. Ibid.

46. Independent States in the World, Fact Sheet, Bureau of Intelligence
    and Research, U.S. Department of State, July 29, 2009; available at:
    http://www.state.gov/s/inr/rls/4250.htm [accessed July 29, 2010].

47. Michael White, "Barack Obama snubs Gordon Brown over pri-
    vate talks," *Guardian*, September 24, 2010; available at: http://
    www.guardian.co.uk/politics/2009/sep/23/barack-obama-gordon-
    brown-talks [accessed July 29, 2010].

48. Hannah Strange, "Latin America backs Argentina in Falklands
    row with Britain," *Times*, February 23, 2010; available at: http://
    www.timesonline.co.uk/tol/news/world/us_and_americas/arti-
    cle7037976.ece [accessed July 29, 2010].

49. "President Obama's Refusal to Back Britain on the Falklands is a
    Disgrace," The Foundry Heritage Foundation, February 25, 2010;
    available at: http://blog.heritage.org/2010/02/25/president-obama's-
    refusal-to-back-britain-on-falklands-is-disgrace/ [accessed July 29,
    2010].

50. "Dalai Lama's quiet White House exit foiled," Brian Williams,
    NBC Nightly News, NBC, February 19, 2010. available at:
    http://www.msnbc.msn.com/id/21134540/vp/35488280#3548828
    0 [accessed August 5, 2010].

51. Mail Foreign Service, "Joe Biden's snub to Netanyahu as he
    arrives 90 minutes late for dinner in middle of row with Israel
    over West Bank houses," March 10, 2010; available at: http://
    www.dailymail.co.uk/news/worldnews/article-1256936/Joe-Biden-
    snubs-Israeli-PM-surprise-announcement-build-homes-war-won-
    land-U-S-vice-presidents-visit.html [accessed July 29, 2010].

52. Adrian Blomfield, "Obama snubbed Netanyahu for dinner with
    Michelle and the girls, Israelis claim," *Telegralph*, March 25,

2010; available at: http://www.telegraph.co.uk/news/worldnews/northamerica/usa/barackobama/7521220/Obama-snubbed-Netanyahu-for-dinner-with-Michelle-and-the-girls-Israelis-claim.html [accessed July 29, 2010].

53. "Text of Democrat Barack Obama's prepared remarks for a rally on Tuesday in St. Paul, Minn., as released by his campaign," Breitbart.com, June 3, 2008; available at http://www.breitbart.com/article.php?id=d912vd200&show_article=1 [accessed August 5, 2010].

54. Richard Esposito, Pierre Thomas, and Jack Date, "Recruiter Shooting Suspect Under FBI Investigation," ABC News, June 1, 2009; available at: http://abcnews.go.com/Politics/story?id=7730637&page=1 [accessed July 29, 2010].

55. Peter Bergen, "The Terrorists Among Us," Foreign Policy, November 19, 2009; available at: http://www.foreignpolicy.com/articles/2009/11/18/the_terrorists_among_us?page=0,0 [accessed July 29, 2010].

56. Richard Esposito, Pierre Thomas, and Jack Date, "Recruiter Shooting Suspect Under FBI Investigation," ABC News, June 1, 2010; available at: http://abcnews.go.com/Politics/story?id=7730637&page=1 [accessed July 29, 2010].

57. "No Bomb Found Inside Van Abandoned in New York's Time Square," FOXNews.com, December 30, 2009; available at: http://www.foxnews.com/us/2009/12/30/bomb-inside-van-abandoned-new-yorks-times-square/ [accessed July 29, 2010].

58. Liam Stack, "Yemen ties of Northwest bomber Umar Farouk Abdulmutallab test Guantanamo plans," Christian Science Monitor, December 29, 2009; available at: http://www.csmonitor.com/World/terrorism-security/2009/1229/Yemen-ties-of-Northwest-bomber-Umar-Farouk-Abdulmutallab-test-Guantanamo-plans [accessed July 29, 2010].

59. Chris McGreal, "Yemen warns of hundreds more al-Qaida operatives in country and asks for help," Guardian, December 30,

2009; available at: http://www.guardian.co.uk/world/2009/dec/29/
yemen-al-quaida-intelligence [accessed July 29, 2010].

60. Tom Hays, "Officials: Replica shows NY bomb could have killed,"
Associated Press, July 20, 2010; available at: http://news. yahoo.com/
s/ap/us_times_square_car_bomb [accessed August 5, 2010].

61. "We Need a Wartime President," *Newsweek*; available at: http://
www.newsweek.com/id/143747/page/1 [accessed July 29, 2010].

62. Associated Press, "Source: U.S. knew of would-be airliner
bomber's terror ties," Haaretz.com, December 26, 2009; available
at: http://www.haaretz.com/news/source-u-s-knew-of-would-be-
airliner-bomber-s-terror-ties-1.1375 [accessed July 29, 2010].

63. Michael Kirkland, "Berwick, new Medicare chief, an admirer of
an imperfect NHS," UPI.com, July 11, 2010; available at:
http://www.upi.com/Top_News/US/2010/07/11/Berwick-new-
Medicare-chief-an-admirer-of-an-imperfect-NHS/UPI-
86101278844200/ [accessed August 5, 2010].

64. "Obama 2nd Circuit Nominee Abused Power, Helped Rapist and
Serial Killer," RedState.com, April 29, 2010; available at:
http://www.redstate.com/hogan/2010/04/29/obama-2nd-circuit-
nominee-abused-power-helped-rapist-and-serial-killer/ [accessed
August 5, 2010].

65. William Letts IV and James Sears, *Queering Elementary Education: Advancing the Dialogue about Sexualities and Schooling*
(Rowman & Littlefield Publishers, Inc., 1999).

66. Editorial, "At the President's Pleasure," *Washington Times*, September 28, 2009; available at: http://washingtontimes.com/news/
2009/sep/28/at-the-presidents-pleasure/ [accessed July 29, 2010].

67. Sam Theodosopoulos, "Fox News Notes Communist Past of the
'Green Jobs' Czar," NewsBusters.org, July 10, 2009; available at:
http://newsbusters.org/blogs/sam-theodosopoulos/2009/07/10/fox-
news-notes-communist-past-green-jobs-czar [accessed July 29, 2010].

68. Amanda Carpenter, "Green jobs czar signed 'truther' statement in
2004," *Washington Times*, September 3, 2009; available at:
http://www.washingtontimes.com/weblogs/back-story/2009/sep/

03/green-jobs-czar-signed-truther-statement-in-2004/ [accessed August 4, 2010].

69. Posted by Erick Erickson, "Barack Obama's Green Jobs Czar Van Jones: White People are Polluters and Republicans are A—holes," RedState.com, September 3, 2009; available at: http://www.redstate.com/erick/2009/09/03/barack-obamas-green-jobs-czar-van-jones-white-people-are-polluters-and-republicans-are-a-holes/ [accessed July 29, 2010].

70. "Obama's Communist Green Jobs Czar Van Jones Says Republicans Are 'A**holes,'" Brietbart TV; available at: http://www.breitbart.tv/obamas-communist-green-jobs-czar-van-jones-says-republicans-are-assholes/ [accessed July 29, 2010].

71. Glenn Greenwald, "Obama Confidant's Spine-Chilling Proposal," Salon.com, January 15, 2010; available at: http://www.salon.com/news/opinion/glenn_greenwald/2010/01/15/sunstein [accessed July 29, 2010].

72. Ibid.

CHAPTER 3

1. Samuel Adams, "Letter to James Warren" in *The Writings of Samuel Adams* (G. P. Putnam's Son, 1908).

2. "Barack Obama sought the New Party's endorsement knowing it was a radical left organization," Posted by RedState.com, 2008; available at: http://archive.redstate.com/stories/elections/2008/barack_obama_sought_the_new_partys_endorsement_knowing_it_was_a_radical_left_organization [accessed July 29, 2010].

3. Fusion is generally prohibited by law in the majority of states, but it survives in a few states in various forms. Connecticut, Delaware, Idaho, Mississippi, New York, South Carolina, and Vermont have some form of fusion. New Hampshire has fusion elections if write-in candidates win primary nominations.

4. Stanley Kurtz, "Inside Obama's Acorn," *National Review* Online, May 29, 2008; available at: http://article.nationalreview.com/358910/inside-obamas-acorn/stanley-kurtz [accessed July 29, 2010].

CHAPTER 4

1. Charles Brancelen Flood, 1864: *Lincoln at the Gates of History* (New York: Simon and Schuster, 2009)
2. James Otis, speech at Law Boston Sugar Act of 1765.
3. Randall G. Holcombe, "Federal Government Growth Before the New Deal," September 1, 1997; available at: http://www.indepen dent.org/publications/article.asp?id=360 [accessed July 15, 2010].
4. "United States Federal and State Local Government Spending," Government Spending Details; data available at: http://www.us governmentspending.com/year1910_0.html [accessed July 15, 2010].
5. Calculations: Fiscal Year 2010 total federal spending of $3.618 trillion comes from Congressional Budget Office, "An Analysis of the President's Budgetary Proposals for Fiscal Year 2011," March 2010, p. 2; available at: http://www.cbo.gov/ftpdocs/112xx/doc11280/03-24-APB.pdf [accessed July 15, 2010]; see also, Population estimates, U.S. Census Bureau; available at: http://www.census.gov/popest/national/NA-EST2009-01.html [accessed July 15, 2010].
6. Fact Sheets: Taxes, "History of the U.S. Tax System," United States Department of the Treasury; available at: http://www.ustreas.gov/education/fact-sheets/taxes/ustax.shtml [accessed July 15, 2010].
7. Budget of the U.S. Government, Fiscal Year 2011, Historical Tables, pp. 24–25.
8. "Total Budgeted Government Spending Expenditure GDP—CHARTS—Deficit Debt," USGovernmentSpending.com, July 9, 2010; available at: http://www.usgovernmentspending.com/down-chart_gs.php?year=1903_2010&view=1&expand=&units=p&fy=fy11&chart=F0total&bar=0&stack=1&size=l&title=US%20Go vernment%20Spending%20As%20Percent%20Of%20GDP&sta te=US&color=c&local=s [accessed July 15, 2010].
9. Calvin Woodward, "PROMISES, PROMISES: Obama tax pledge up in smoke," Breitbart, April 1, 2010; available at: http://

www.breitbart.com/article.php?id=D979POSG0 [accessed July 15, 2010].

10. Average Federal Taxes by Income Group, Congressional Budget Office, June 2010; available at: http://www.cbo.gov/publications/collections/collections.cfm?collect=13 [accessed July 15, 2010].

11. Ibid; data available at: http://cbo.gov/publications/collections/tax/2009/tax_liability_shares.pdf) [accessed July 15, 2010].

12. Budget of the U.S. Government, Fiscal Year 2011, Historical Tables, 25.

13. US Government Spending as percent of GDP, USGovernmentSpending.com, July 9, 2010; available at: http://www.usgovernmentspending.com/downchart_gs.php?year=1903_2010&view=1&expand=&units=p&fy=fy11&chart=F0total&bar=0&stack=1&size=l&title=US%20Government%20Spending%20As%20Percent%20Of%20GDP&state=US&color=c&local=s [accessed July 15, 2010].

14. Daily Policy Digest, "Europe's VAT Lessons: Rates Start Low and Increase, While Income Tax Rates Stay High," National Center for Policy Analysis, April 15, 2010; available at: http://www.ncpa.org/sub/dpd/index.php?Article_ID=19222 [accessed July 15, 2010].

15. Brutus, *The AntiFederalist Papers*, No. 33.

16. Question and Answer, FactCheck.org, June 29, 2008; available at: http://www.factcheck.org/askfactcheck/whats_the_percentage_breakdown_of_the_governments.html [accessed July 15, 2010].

17. Fact Sheet: Taxes, "History of the U.S. Tax System," U.S. Department of the Treasury; available at: http://www.ustreas.gov/education/fact-sheets/taxes/uustax.shtml [accessed August 5, 2010].

CHAPTER 5

1. Thomas Jefferson to John Wayles Eppes, 1813. ME 13:169; available at: http://etext.virginia.edu/jefferson/quotations/jeff1340.htm

[accessed July 22, 2010].

2. *Wickard* v. *Filburn*, 317 U.S. 111 (1942).

3. Video, "Judiciary hearing on Elena Kagan: Dr. Coburn's Remarks (Day 2)," posted by Senator Coburn on June 29, 2010; available at: http://www.youtube.com/watch?v=Tgdetb9A4aY&feature= channel [accessed July 22, 2010].

4. George B. Galloway, *History of the United States House of Representatives* (Washington, DC: US Government Printing Office, 1962), 110.

5. Ibid.; see also, "Guide to Congress," *Congressional Quarterly*, Second Edition, 1976, p. 460.

6. Norman J. Ornstein et. al, "Vital Statistics on Congress," *American Enterprise Institute*, 1984–85, pp. 121–22, 124.

7. Budget of the U.S. Government, Fiscal Year 1914.

8. Allen Wastler, "Congress' Pension: Nice and Secure," CNN-money.com, January 20, 2006; available at: http://money.cnn.com/ 2006/01/20/commentary/wastler/wastler/index.htm [accessed July 28, 2010].

9. Erika Lovley, "2,000 House Staffers Make Six Figures," *Politico*, March 26, 2010; available at: http://www.politico.com/news/stories/0310/35050.html [accessed July 22, 2010].

10. Capitol Questions, CSPAN.com, November 13, 2000; available at: http://www.c-span.org/questions/weekly35.asp [accessed July 22, 2010]; see also, "About the Library," Library of Congress; available at: http://www.loc.gov/about/generalinfo.html#2009 _at_a_glance [accessed July 22, 2010].

11. Erika Lovley, "2,000 House Staffers Make Six Figures," *Politico*, March 26, 2010; available at: http://www.politico.com/news/stories/0310/35050.html [accessed July 22, 2010].

12. Dan Mitchell, "The Number of Congressional Staff is the Real Problem," Cato, March 30, 2010; available at: http://www.cato-at-liberty.org/2010/03/30/the-number-of-congressional-staff-is-the-real-problem/ [accessed July 22, 2010].

13. Mark Brisnow, "Congress: An Insider's Look at the Mess on Capitol Hill," *Newsweek*, January 4, 1988.

14. George B. Galloway, *History of the United States House of Representatives*, 113.

15. David Freddoso, "Waxman Cancels Obamacare CEO Hearings," *Washington Examiner*, April 14, 2010; available at: http://www.washingtonexaminer.com/opinion/blogs/beltway-confidential/Waxman-cancels-health-care-CEO-hearing-90853384.html [accessed July 22, 2010].

CHAPTER 6

1. William B. Irvine, "'Brutus': Anti-Federalist Hero," *The Wall Street Journal*, February 6, 1987.

2. Congress of the United States Congressional Budget, "An Analysis of the President's Budgetary Proposals for Fiscal Year 2011," March 2010; available at: http://www.cbo.gov/ftpdocs/112xx/doc11280/03-24-apb.pdf [accessed July 22, 2010].

3. "ObamaCare's Real Price Tag," *Wall Street Journal*, August 6, 2009; available at: http://online.wsj.com/article/SB100014240529702036092045743146220755560890.html [accessed July 22, 2010].

4. Carmen M. Reinhart and Kenneth S. Rogoff, *This Time Is Different: Eight Centuries of Financial Folly* (Princeton University Press, 2009); see also, Daniel Fisher, "The Global Debt Bomb," *Forbes Magazine*, February 8, 2010.

5. David Walker, "Call this a crisis? Just wait," *Fortune Magazine*, October 30, 2008; available at: http://money.cnn.com/2008/10/28/magazines/fortune/babyboomcrisis_walker.fortune/index.htm [accessed August 5, 2010].

6. "2010 Index for Economic Freedom," Heritage Foundation; available at: http://www.heritage.org/index/ [accessed July 22, 2010].

7. "U.S. debt to rise to $19.6 trillion by 2015," Reuters, June 8, 2010; available at: http://www.reuters.com/article/idUSN0884

62520100608 [accessed July 28, 2010].

8. There are 118 million households in the United States in 2010.

9. "The Budget and Economic Outlook: An Update, August 2009," Congressional Budget Office; available at: http://www.cbo.gov/ftp-docs/105xx/doc10521/2009BudgetUpdate_Summary.pdf [accessed July 22, 2010].

10. Congress of the United States Congressional Budget, "An Analysis of the President's Budgetary Proposals for Fiscal Year 2011," March 2010; available at: http://www.cbo.gov/ftpdocs/112xx/doc11280/03-24-apb.pdf [accessed July 22, 2010].

11. Pamela Villarreal, "Social Security and Medicare Projections: 2009," National Center for Policy Analysis, June 11, 2009; available at: http://www.ncpa.org/pub/ba662 [accessed July 22, 2010].

12. Memo, "A Message from the Secretary of Treasury," Department of the Treasury, p. 158; available at: http://www.fms.treas.gov/fr/09frusg/09frusg.pdf [accessed July 22, 2010].

13. "The Budget and Economic Outlook: Fiscal Years 2010 to 2020," Congress of the United States Congressional Budget Office; available at: http://www.cbo.gov/ftpdocs/108xx/doc10871/01-26-Outlook.pdf [accessed July 22, 2010].

14. Congress of the United States Congressional Budget, "An Analysis of the President's Budgetary Proposals for Fiscal Year 2011," March 2010; available at: http://www.cbo.gov/ftpdocs/112xx/doc11280/03-24-apb.pdf [accessed July 22, 2010].

CHAPTER 7

1. Adam Smith, *Wealth of Nations* (Prometheus Books, 1991).

2. "The Career of Robert M. LaFollette," Wisconsin Historical Society; available at: http://www.wisconsinhistory.org/turningpoints/tp-035/ [accessed July 29, 2010].

3. Brian Riedl, "Federal Spending by the Numbers 2010," Heritage Foundation, June 1, 2010; available at: http://www.heritage.org/research/reports/2010/06/federal-spending-by-the-numbers-2010

[accessed July 29, 2010].

4. Budget of the United States Government, pp. 5-351990.

5. James T. Bennett and Thomas J. DiLorenzo, "Poverty, Politics, and Jurisprudence: Illegalities at the Legal Services Corporation," Cato Institute, Policy Analysis, February 26, 1985; available at: http://www.cato.org/pubs/pas/pa049.html [accessed August 5, 2010].

6. Chris Edwards, "Federal aid to the States: Historical Cause of Government Growth & Bureaucracy," Cato Policy Analysis 3593, May 22, 2007; available at: http://www.cato.org/pub_display.php?pub_id=8246 [accessed July 29, 2010].

7. Ibid.

8. Ibid.

9. Ibid.

10. Ibid.

11. *The Antifederalist Papers*, No. 62.

12. Tom Walls, "Claude Pepper's Life and Death," afn.org; available at: http://www.afn.org/~afn62971/pepper.html [accessed July 29, 2010].

13. Scott Whitlock, "After Week of Silence: Network Morning Shows Finally Cover Pelosi Plane-gate," NewsBusters.com, February 8, 2007; available at: http://newsbusters.org/node/10702 [accessed July 29, 2010].

14. See George Orwell, *1984* (Signet Classics, 1961).

CHAPTER 8

1. Frederick Bastiat, *The Law*, 1850.

2. Report to Congressional Requesters, "Low-Income Home Energy Assistance Program: Greater Fraud Prevention Controls are Needed," Government Accountability Office, June 2010; available at: http://www.gao.gov/new.items/d10621.pdf [accessed July 30, 2010].

3. Spencer Hsu, "Homeland Security," in "2010 Budget Details: Agency by Agency," *Washington Post*; available at: http://

www.washingtonpost.com/wp-srv/politics/budget2010/
agency_by_agency_050709.html [accessed July 13, 2010].

4. Carrie Johnson, "Justice," in "2010 Budget Details: Agency by
    Agency," *Washington Post*; available at: http://www.washington
    post.com/wp-srv/politics/budget2010/
    agency_by_agency_050709.html [accessed July 13, 2010].

5. U.S. Department of State, "The Budget of the United States Gov-
    ernment for Fiscal Year 2010," submitted by the President under
    section 1105 of title 31, United States Code, fiscal year 2010
    begins on October 1, 2009.

6. "All-Purpose Table—FY 2008-2010," Administration for Chil-
    dren and Families; data available at: http://www.acf.hhs.gov/pro
    grams/olab/budget/2010/fy2010apt_508.pdf [accessed July 13,
    2010].

7. Calculated as 141 countries of 211 countries with reliable esti-
    mates of GDP at less than 50 billion, "The World Factbook,"
    Central Intelligence Agency, updated bi-weekly; available at:
    https://www.cia.gov/library/publications/the-world-factbook/
    fields/2195.html?countryName=&countryCode=&regionCode=
    %3E# [accessed July 13, 2010].

8. Tad DeHaven, "Greek Rail and Amtrak," Cato "Downsizing the
    Federal Government," June 2010; available at: http://
    www.downsizinggovernment.org/greek-rail-and-amtrak [accessed
    July 30, 2010].

9. Chris Edwards, "Ten Reasons to Cut Farm Subsidies," Cato, June
    28, 2007; available at: http://www.cato.org/pub_display.php?
    pub_id=8459 [accessed July 30, 2010].

10. Ibid.

11. Mitzi Ayala, "Farm Subsidies Yield Costly Harvest," *Wall Street
    Journal*, June 4, 1987, editorial page.

12. Chris Edwards, "Agricultural Subsidies," Cato Institute, June
    2009; available at http://www.downsizinggovernment.org/agricul
    ture/subsidies [accessed August 5, 2010].

13. Richard Morrison, "Kerry-Lieberman Bill a Huge Payoff to Big Business," CEI News Release, May 11, 2010; available at: http://cei.org/news-releases/kerry-graham-lieberman-bill-huge-payoff-big-business [accessed July 30, 2010].

14. Letter from Tom Coburn to Alan Simpson and Erskine Bowles, May 18, 2010.

15. Chris Edwards, "Government Cost Overruns," Cato, Downsizing the Federal Government, March 9,2010; available at: http://www.downsizinggovernment.org/government-cost-overruns [accessed July 30, 2010].

16. Tim Carrington, "Air Force Renews Campaign to Scrap Fairchild Industries' T-46 trainer Jet," *Wall Street Journal*, December 10, 1986.

17. "Goodbye, Washington," *Wall Street Journal*, December 10, 1987, editorial page.

CHAPTER 9

1. Commonly attributed to George Washington.

2. Trust Fund Data, Social Security Online; available at: http://www.ssa.gov/OACT/ProgData/fundFAQ.html#n2 [accessed July 30, 2010].

3. Trustees of the Federal Old-Age and Survivors Insurance and Disability Insurance Funds, "The 2001 Annual Report of the board of Trustees of the Federal Old-Age and Survivors Insurance and the Federal Disability Insurance Trust Funds," Social Security Administration, March 19, 2001; available at: http://www.ssa.gov/OACT/TR/TR01/tr01.pdf [accessed August 3, 2010].

4. History, "Life Expectancy for Social Security," Social Security Online; available at: http://www.ssa.gov/history/lifeexpect.html [accessed July 30, 2010].

5. Jeanne Sahadi, Social Security "A plan both parties can love (and hate)" CNN Money, June 19, 2006; available at: http://money.cnn.com/2006/06/19/retirement/lms_proposal/ [accessed July 30, 2010].

6. Paul Ryan, "Roadmap Solutions: Description of the Legislation,"

A Roadmap for America's Future; available at: http://
www.roadmap.republicans.budget.house.gov/solution/roadmap-
solutions.htm [accessed July 30, 2010].

7. Ibid.

8. José Piñera, "How We Privatized Social Security in Chile," *The
Freeman: Ideas On Liberty*, July 1997; available at: http://
www.hacer.org/pdf/socsec.pdf [accessed July 30, 2010].

9. Editorial, "Federal Mutual Fund," *Investors Business Daily*, May
20, 2010; available at: http://www.investors.com/NewsAnd-
Analysis/Article.aspx?id=533718 [accessed July 30, 2010].

10. John C. Goodman, "Goodbye Employer-Sponsored Insurance,"
Wall Street Journal, May 21, 2010; available at: http://
online.wsj.com/article/NA_WSJ_PUB:SB100014240527487038
80304575236602943319816.html [accessed July 30, 2010].

11. Ibid.

12. Pascal Fletcher, "Florida says challenge to healthcare reform widens,"
Reuters.com, April 7, 2010; available at: http://www. reuters.com/
article/idUSTRE6363NL20100407 [accessed August 5, 2010].

13. Steven Hayward and Erik Peterson, "The Medicare Monster: A
Cautionary Tale," *Reason Magazine*, January 1993; available at:
http://reason.com/archives/1993/01/01/the-medicare-monster
[accessed July 30, 2010].

14. "Health Insurance in the United States," Economic History Association; available at: http://eh.net/encyclopedia/article/thomas-
son.insurance.health.us [accessed July 30, 2010].

CHAPTER 10

1. Dr. Jim Cornehls, "The USA Patriot Act and Censorship," Sept 24,
2003, pg 16; available at: http://docs.google.com/viewer?a=v&q=
cache:S6UTM xY96bgJ: www.uta.edu/library/cornehls/the_usa_
patriot_act_and_censorship.pdf+did+Thomas+Paine+write+it+is+
the+responsibility+of+the+patriot+to+protect+his+country+form+
its+government&hl=en&gl=us&pid=bl&srcid=ADGEEShJ8SXnk

Q0Yfsie8A7Q_0wxDLq5J_JgHWi8PVwvH04NT9jkrIsDr6e6sjP
FcUAVUxifrr0H_mTMBG-1Oi0XO7KX03UpgasqZDnOPEWEE
MDCMBzpE633IrFL35iB3Q9kwENJjK6t&sig=AHIEtbSkpZBxl
XNxMWa0VdRwu1_giXCWew [accessed July 29, 2010].

2. "Flat proportional income taxes 2010—From 1 to 25 countries in
    16 years," Ohrid Institute for Economic Strategies and Interna-
    tional Affairs;" available at: http://oi.org.mk/upload/Flat-propo
    tional-income-taxes.pdf [accessed August 2, 2010].

3. "Red Ink Rising: A Call to Action to Stem the Mounting Federal
    Debt," The Peterson-Pew Commission on Budget Reform, Dec.
    2009, pp 16-17; available at: www.budgetreform.org [accessed
    August 4, 2010].

4. Jocelyne Bourgon, "Program Review: A Canadian Case Study,"
    May 12, 2009; available at: http://pgionline.com/documents/
    ifg_program_review.pdf [accessed July 29, 2010].

5. Daniel Mitchell, The Heritage Foundation, "The Impact of Gov-
    ernment Spending on Economic Growth," March 2005; available
    at: http://www.heritage.org/Research/Reports/2005/03/The-Imp
    act-of-Government-Spending-on-Economic-Growth [accessed July
    29, 2010].

6. Maurice McTigue, "Rolling Back Government: Lessons from New
    Zealand," Imprimis, 2004.

7. Organization for Economic Co-operation and Development,
    "Annex Table 25: General Government Total Outlays," Economic
    Outlook No. 76. Nov 2004; available at http://www.oecd.org/
    document/61/0,3343,en_2649_34573_2483901_1_1_1_1,00.htm
    l [accessed August 5, 2010].

8. "Permanently repeal the estate tax," Daily Local News, May 27,
    2010; available at: http://www.dailylocal.com/articles/2010/05/27/
    opinion/srv0000008375483.txt [accessed July 29, 2010].

9. Base Realignment and Closure (BRAC), GlobalSecurity.org; avail-
    able at: http://www.globalsecurity.org/military/facility/brac.htm
    [accessed July 29, 2010].

10. Vocational Education State Grants, Program Assessment, Expect-More.gov; available at: http://www.whitehouse.gov/omb/expect moresummary/10000212.2002.html [accessed August 5, 2010].

11. Community Development Block Grant (Formula), Program Assessment, ExpectMore.gov; available at: http://www.white house. gov/omb/expectmore/summary/10001161.2003.html [accessed August 5, 2010].

CHAPTER 11

1. Senator John Sharp Williams, *Thomas Jefferson: His Permanent Influence on American Institutions,* 49 (1913). Lecture delivered at Columbia University, New York City, 1912.

2. Gerald Scully, "Future Tax Policies Should Maximize Economic Growth," NCPA, November 21, 2006; available at: http://www.ncpa.org/sub/dpd/index.php?Article_ID=13879# [accessed July 29, 2010].

3. Gerald Scully, "What Is the Optimal Size of Government in the United States?" NCPA, November 1994; available at: http://www.ncpa.org/pdfs/st188.pdf, p. 7 [accessed July 29, 2010]. As noted in one of Scully's reports, government expenditures are usually expressed as a share of gross domestic product (GDP) but gross national product (GNP) was used until the 1980s. GNP and GDP figures differ slightly, but not enough to create a serious distortion.

4. Gerald Scully, "Future Tax Policies Should Maximize Economic Growth," NCPA, November 21, 2006; available at http://www.ncpa.org/sub/dpd/index.php?Article_ID=13879# [accessed July 29, 2010].

5. Ibid.

6. Daniel Mitchell, "The Impact of Government Spending on Economic Growth," Heritage Foundation, March 15, 2005; available at: http://www.heritage.org/Research/Reports/2005/03/The-Im pact-of-Government-Spending-on-Economic-Growth [accessed July 29, 2010].

7. James Gwartney, Randall Holcombe, and Robert Lawson, "The Scope of Government and the Wealth of Nations," *The Cato Journal,*(1998)18.2: 163–90.

CHAPTER 12

1. George Mason, debate with James Madison, the Federal Convention, June 11, 1787; text available at: http://avalon.law.yale.edu/18th_century/debates_611.asp [accessed July 29, 2010].
2. Kate Mason Rowland, *Life and Correspondence of George Mason*, Volume II (New York: Putnam's Sons, 1892).
3. Richard Labunski, Constitutional Commentary, "The second convention movement, 1787-1789," *Constitutional Commentary*, September 22, 2007; article available at: http://www.highbeam.com/doc/1G1-190748170.html [accessed July 29, 2010].
4. Russell L. Captain, *Constitutional Brinkmanship: Amending the Constitution by National Convention* (NY: Oxford University Press, 1988), 79.
5. Ratings Of Congress ACU, 1979 ACU HOUSE VOTE DESCRIPTIONS, Line 19; available at: http://www.conservative.org/ratings/ratingsarchive/1979/desc_hse.html [accessed July 29, 2010].
6. Russell L. Caplan, *Constitutional Brinkmanship: Amending the Constitution by National Convention* (New York: Oxford University Press 1988), 81–82.
7. Another dimension of this battle, as John Noonan, a former constitutional law professor and federal judge, pointed out, had to do with popular discipline of the federal courts.
8. Congressmen Jeb Hensarling, Mike Pence, and John Campbell, "Spending Limit Amendment"; available at: http://www.gop.gov/sla [accessed July 29, 2010].
9. Thomas Jefferson to John Taylor, 1798.

CHAPTER 13

1. Abraham Lincoln, "July 4th Message to Congress," July 4, 1861;

available at: http://millercenter.org/scripps/archive/speeches/detail/ 3508 [accessed August 6, 2010].

2. Information on Lamar's SAFE Act; available at: http:// www.opencongress.org/bill/111-h5323/show [accessed July 29, 2010].

3. Dennis Cauchon, "Benefits widen public, private workers' pay gap," *USA Today*, April 10, 2009; available at: http:// www.usatoday.com/money/workplace/2009-04-09-compensation_N.htm [accessed July 29, 2010].

4. Dennis Cauchon, "For feds, more get 6-figure salaries," *USA Today*, December 11, 2009; available at: http://www.usatoday. com/news/washington/2009-12-10-federal-pay-salaries_N.htm [accessed July 29, 2010].

5. Historical Workforce Tables, U.S. Office of Personnel Management, http://www.opm.gov/feddata/HistoricalTables/TotalGovernmentSince1962.asp [accessed July 29, 2010]

6. Pension Benefit Guaranty Corporation is a federal corporation created by the Employee Retirement Income Security Act of 1974. It currently protects the pensions of more than 44 million American workers and retirees in more than 29,000 private single-employer and multiemployer defined benefit pension plans. PBGC receives no funds from general tax revenues. Operations are financed by insurance premiums set by Congress and paid by sponsors of defined benefit plans, investment income, assets from pension plans trusteed by PBGC, and recoveries from the companies formerly responsible for the plans. Available at: http://www.pbgc.gov/ [accessed August 6, 2010].

7. Rene Girard, "'Cheap Tomatoes' viral email on Mexican immigrants in CA schools is based upon a true story," *San Diego Christianity & Culture Examiner*, July 23, 2010.

8. Daniel Millimet, Rusty Tchernis, and Muna Hussain, "School Nutrition Programs and the Incidence of Childhood Obesity," Indiania University, CAEPR, August 7, 2007; available at: http://

ideas.repec.org/p/inu/caeprp/2007014.html [accessed July 29, 2010].

9. See "Barack Obama Campaign Promise No. 308: Fully fund the Community Development Block Grant (CDBG)," PolitiFact; available at: http://www.politifact.com/truth-o-meter/promises/promise/308/fully-fund-the-community-development-block-grant/ [accessed July 29, 2010].

10. Tad DeHaven, "Community Development," CATO, June 2009; available at: http://www.downsizinggovernment.org/hud/commu-nity-development [accessed July 29, 2010].

11. The Davis-Bacon and Related Acts (DBRA); available at: http://www.dol.gov/compliance/laws/comp-dbra.htm [accessed July 29, 2010].

12. Another dimension of this battle, as John Noonan, a former con-stitutional law professor and federal judge, pointed out, had to do with popular discipline of the federal courts.

13. Rules of the House of Representatives, 110th Congress, March 2008; available at: http://www.rules.house.gov/ruleprec/110th.pdf [accessed August 6, 2010].

14. Congressional Budget Office, "List of Unauthorized Appropria-tions and Expiring Authorizations," January 2010; available at http://www.cbo.gov/ftpdocs/108xx/doc10882/01-19-UAEA_House.pdf [accessed August 6, 2010].

15. Bill Heniff Jr. "House Rules Changes Affecting the Congressional Budget Process Made at the Beginning of the 110th Congress," CRS Report For Congress, August 30, 2007; available at: http://budget.house.gov/crs-reports/RL34149.pdf [accessed August 6, 2010].

16. Data available at: http://www.downsizinggovernment.org/ [accessed July 29, 2010].

17. Brian Riedl, biography; available at: http://www.heritage.org/About/Staff/R/Brian-Riedl [accessed July 29, 2010].

18. Scott A. Hodge, biography; available at: http://www.taxfounda tion.org/staff/show/5.html [accessed July 29, 2010].

19. Tracie Sharp, biography; available at: http://www.spn.org/about/
    pageID.48/default.asp [accessed July 29, 2010].

20. "Who is Grover Norquist?" Americans for Tax Reform; available
    at: http://www.atr.org/grover-norquist-a3016 [accessed July 29,
    2010].

21. "About Freedomworks: Chairman Dick Armey," FreedomWorks;
    available at: http://www.freedomworks.org/about/chairman-dick-
    armey [accessed July 29, 2010]. See also, Matt Kibbe biography,
    FreedomWorks; available at: http://www.freedomworks.org/matt-
    kibbe-biography [accessed July 29, 2010].

22. Duane Parde, biography; available at: http://www.ntu.org/about-
    ntu/staff/duane-parde.html [accessed July 29, 2010].

23. Tom Schatz, biography; available at: http://councilfor.cagw.org/
    site/PageServer?pagename=about_schatz [accessed July 29, 2010].

24. NTLC's Board of Adviors; available at: http://www.limittaxes.
    com/about-ntlc/board-of-advisors/ [accessed July 29, 2010].

25. "About ACU," the American Conservative Union; available at:
    http://www.conservative.org/about-acu/ [accessed July 29, 2010].

26. "About the Free Congress Foundation;" available at: http://
    www.freecongress.org/aboutfcf.html [accessed July 29, 2010].

27. "About Americans for Prosperity;" available at: http://
    www.americansforprosperity.org/about [accessed July 29, 2010].

28. Lindy L. Paull, quoted in Jim Powell, "Government: More Incom-
    petent than Ever," *The Freeman*, May 2010; available at: http://
    www.thefreemanonline.org/featured/government-more-incompe-
    tent-than-ever/# [accessed July 29, 2010].

29. National Taxpayer Advocate, 2008 Annual Report to Congress, Vol-
    ume 1, December 31, 2008; available at: http://www.irs.gov/pub/irs-
    utl/08_tas_arc_intro_toc_msp.pdf, p. 4 [accessed July 29, 2010].

30. Tax Data, The Tax Foundation; available at: http://www.taxfoun
    dation.org/taxdata/show/386.html [accessed July 29, 2010].

31. Cokie Roberts, "Cokie Roberts says government accounts for 40
    percent of GDP" Politi-Fact.com, Oct 2009; available at:

http://www.politifact.com/truth-o-meter/statements/2009/oct/06/
cokie-roberts/cokie-roberts-says-government-accounts-40-percent-
[accessed August 6, 2010].

32. Chris Atkins and Scott Hodge, "U.S. Lagging Behind OECD Corporate Tax Trends," The Tax Foundation Fiscal Fact, May 5,
2006; available at: http://www.taxfoundation.org/news/show/
1466.html [accessed August 6, 2010].

33. Dwight L. Schwab Jr., "Six months to go until largest tax hike in
U.S. history," *Examiner*, July 13, 2010; available at: http://
www.examiner.com/x-11780-Bay-Area-Moderate-Conservative-
Examiner~y2010m7d13-Six-months-to-go-until-largest-tax-hike-
in-US-history [July 29, 2010].

34. Dan Mitchell, "The Deadly Impact of the Death Tax," BigGov-
ernment.com, July 16, 2010; available at: http://biggovern-
ment.com/dmitchell/2010/07/16/
the-deadly-impact-of-the-death-tax/ [accessed July 29, 2010].

35. Fred Lucas, "Obama Administration Sends Mixed Message on
VAT as Fiscal Commission Prepares First Meeting,"
CNSNews.com, April 26, 2010; available at: http://
www.cnsnews.com/news/article/64671 [accessed July 29, 2010].

36. Lawrence A. Hunter and Stephen J. Entin, "A Framework For Tax
Reform," Institute for Policy Innovation, January 14, 2005; available at: http://www.ipi.org/ipi%5CIPIPublications.nsf/Publica-
tionLookupFullText/28B082C7EB246EDC86256F8C005774F9
[accessed July 29, 2010].

CHAPTER 14

1. Commonly attributed to Samuel Adams.

2. "The Death of William McKinley," Buffalo History Works; available at: http://www.buffalohistoryworks.com/panamex/assassina-
tion/mcdeath.htm [accessed July 30, 2010].

3. Special Features, "Win the Election of 1912," PBS.org; available
at: http://www.pbs.org/wgbh/amex/wilson/sfeature/sf_election.

html [accessed July 30, 2010].

4. "1992 Presidential General Election Results," uselectionatlas.org; available at: http://uselectionatlas.org/RESULTS/national.php? f=0&year=1992 [accessed July 30, 2010].

5. Special Features, "Win the Election of 1912," PBS.org; available at: http://www.pbs.org/wgbh/amex/wilson/sfeature/sf_election. html [accessed July 30, 2010].

6. "1992 Presidential General Election Results," uselectionatlas.org; available at: http://uselectionatlas.org/RESULTS/national.php? f=0&year=1992 [accessed July 30, 2010].

7. Jake Gibson, "Utah Republican Sen. Bob Bennett Ousted in Re-election Bid," FOXNews.com, May 8, 2010; available at: http://www.foxnews.com/politics/2010/05/08/sen-bennett-faces-conservative-test-utah/ [accessed July 30, 2010].

8. Liz Sidoti and Jim Davenport, "2010 Primary Results: Utah, South Carolina, North Carolina, Mississippi," *Huffington Post*, June 22, 2010; available at: http://www.huffingtonpost.com/2010/06/22/2010-primary-results-utah_n_620535.html [accessed July 30, 2010].

9. Brendan Farrington, "1 year later, Florida Senate candidate Rubio holds rally at site of Crist/Obama stimulus hug," Associated Press, February 11, 2010; available at: http://www.washingtonexaminer.com/economy/1-year-later-florida-senate-candidate-rubio-holds-rally-at-site-of-cristobama-stimulus-hug-84120177.html [accessed August 6, 2010].

10. Chris Cillizza, "Dick Cheney, Trey Grayson and the Fix endorsement hierarchy," *Washington Post*, The Fix; available at: http://voices.washingtonpost.com/thefix/fix-endorsement-hierarchy/dick-cheney-trey-grayson-and-t.html [accessed July 30, 2010].

CHAPTER 15

1. Sir Winston Churchill, *The Second World War, Vol. 1: The Gathering Storm* (Mariner Books, 1986), 348.

2. "Republican Party Faces Ideological Rifts Ahead of Election Season," Aired July 7, 2010; video available at: http://www.pbs.org/newshour/bb/politics/july-dec10/gop_07-07.html [accessed July 30, 2010].

3. Information related by Attorney Dan Schultz who leads an effort to recruit precinct leaders and writes on the subject regularly at redstate.com.

4. Entry, "Butterfly Effect," Wikipedia.com; available at: http://en.wikipedia.org/wiki/Butterfly_effect [accessed July 13, 2010].

5. Modified from an original post at RedState.com

6. Jon Henke, "Left Watch: 2009 Agenda," The Next Right, blog, posted June 12, 2008; available at: http://www.thenextright.com/jon-henke/left-watch-2009-agenda [accessed July 13, 2010].

7. Chris Bowers, "Legislation That Will Pass With A Democratic Trifecta," Open Left, blog, posted June 11, 2008; available at: http://openleft.com/showDiary.do?diaryId=6303 [accessed July 13, 2010].

8. Letter from Jefferson to James Madison on January 30, 1787. Carved on the wall of Monticello.

INDEX